Hands and How to Read Them

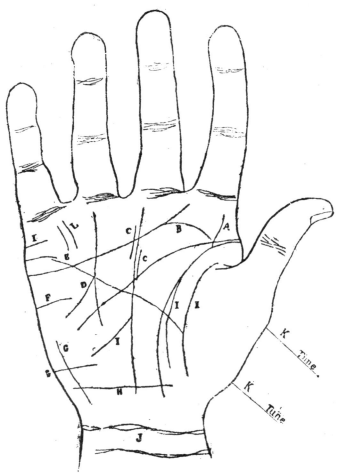

PLATE IV.

MINOR LINES, ANGLES AND RASCETTES.

A.	Ambition Lines.	H.	Line of Intemperance.
B.	Loss of a Friend.	I. I. I. I.	Influence Lines.
C. C.	Fate Line Doubled.	J.	The Rascettes or Bracelets.
D.	Legacy.	K K.	Angles of Music (Time and
E.	Separation or Divorce.		Tune as indicated.)
F.	Enmity Line.	L.	Science Lines.
G. G.	Long Journey or Voyage.		

Hands and How to Read Them

A Popular Guide to Palmistry

By

E. René

With 16 full-page Illustrations

London

C. Arthur Pearson Ltd

Henrietta Street, W.C.

1917

PRYOR PUBLICATIONS
WHITSTABLE AND WALSALL

Specialist in Facsimile Reproductions

Member of
Independent Publishers Guild

75 Dargate Road, Yorkletts, Whitstable,
Kent CT5 3AE, England
Tel. & Fax (01227) 274655
E-mail: alan@pryor-publications.co.uk
www.pryor-publications.co.uk
From the USA Toll Free Phone/Fax
1866 363 9007

Kent Exporter of the Year Awards Winner
Shortlisted
International Business Awards

A full list of publications sent free on request.

SYNOPSIS OF CONTENTS.

PART I.

CHAPTER I
On the Outward Formation of the Hand

CHAPTER II
The Fingers and Palms

CHAPTER III
The Nails and Phalanges

CHAPTER IV
The Mounts and their Attributes

CHAPTER V
On the Principal Lines

CHAPTER VI
Fortune, Health, Marriage and their Lines

GLOSSARY OF TERMS.

The Mounts—The fleshy elevations under the fingers and on the lower part of the hand.

The Phalanges—The three divisions of each finger.

The Percussion—The outward or striking part of the hand from the base of the fourth finger to the wrist.

Hepatica—The name given to the Health or Liver-line (from Hepatic—pertaining to the liver).

The Rascettes or Bracelets—The lines which encircle the wrist.

The Quadrangle—The space between Head and Heart-lines.

The Triangle—The junction of the lines of Head, Life, and Hepatica in the centre of the hand.

Grille—A grating or crossed fagot of small lines.

An "islanded" line—A line which divides into two for a short space and rejoins.

A "feathered" line—Having the appearance of a feather.

A "chained" line—Having the appearance of a chain.

A "waisted" thumb—A thumb which is cut away at each side on the second phalange.

The "Knots"—Enlargement of the finger joints.

Introduction

It is not my intention in the following pages so much to present to the reader a text-book on Palmistry, as to give a general view of the science, showing what may be learned from the study—the practical uses it may be put to—the indications of health, character, and capabilities that appear upon the hand—the timely warnings that are frequently found thereon—and thereby to awaken an interest in the subject of Chirology, and lead to a more exhaustive investigation.

There are various ways in which the study may be instructive and helpful. As an index to character, tastes and proclivities Palmistry may claim to be almost infallible.

The expression of the eyes and face is, to a great extent, under the control of the individual. A man may assume an emotion he does not feel, but his hand betrays him when he is least conscious of it. To the student who seriously and diligently takes up this study, it is a wonderfully interesting and fascinating example of the marvellous intricacies in the workings of the human mind, and physical organism, showing how one acts upon the other.

It has been proved that any injury to the brain affects the lines on the hand, causing them to disappear or become blurred. A cure being established, however, the lines will re-appear, and the inference to be drawn is, that these marks upon the hand are the result of brain-action. Among the most practical uses Palmistry may be put to are—the training of children, and choosing a career for them. A knowledge of the science will teach the parent what is lacking in the child's nature; will point out the qualities that require encouragement, and those that should be repressed. The science is also a guide as regards health; it shows the tendency to certain diseases, inherited or otherwise, the liability to infection, the proneness to accidents, and the inclination to intemperance.

As an aid to the choice of a profession, trade or occupation, it is extremely helpful. It shows what the "subject" is naturally most fitted for, and were it more often applied to this purpose, there would be fewer mistakes made in launching a boy or girl on the ocean of life. The talents and qualities most useful for a future career would be cultivated, and much valuable time saved which is now wasted in teaching the child what will never be of any use to him, worrying his poor little brain with subjects he has really no aptitude for, and neglecting to develop the gifts he possesses. A judicious study of Palmistry would also afford assistance to the medical profession in diagnosing cases, or in tracing hereditary taints, tendencies, and characteristics. Doctors do sometimes examine the hands in certain ailments, but a closer attention to the subject would yield much useful information, not always possible to obtain from the patient by other means. I have included in these pages a few illustrations from personal experience, which carry out in a remarkable manner the "readings" of certain signs, and go some way towards proving that Palmistry is not mere guess-work.

E. RENÉ.

Hands and How to Read Them

CHAPTER I

On the Outward Formation of the Hand

Chiromancy, or the art of reading and foretelling past and future events from the lines on the hand, is ᶜgreat antiquity, and was known to the Ancient Egyptians. Ages ago the Science found a home in India, and it lives among the Hindoos to the present day. The early Romans also practised Chiromancy. In Europe in the seventeenth century Chiromancy died out, but with the discovery of Chirology it has been revived and placed upon a surer and more scientific foundation. Chirology, or the method through which the character, talents, tendencies, and proclivities are perceived on the hand, is of more recent growth, and was first formulated by D'Arpentigny, whose observations and studies were carried on for a period of thirty years before he definitely established his system. This was afterwards elaborated and extended by Adrien Desbarrolles, and subsequently has been taken up, further developed, and practised by well-known living Palmists, at the head of whom may be placed the name of Mrs. St. Hill, president of the London Chirological Society, who, having devoted much time to the study, has more particularly traced out the indications and results of certain diseases, ailments, and the tendencies thereto, in the signs on the hands, only drawing deductions after careful observation and test, Nature's books are within the reach of all, and once we have the key, much may be learned by personal observation, by listening to tales of woe, adventure, sickness, or other experiences, and afterwards examining the hands of the narrator. With a knowledge of where and how to search, we may trace past events, and not infrequently discover the probable consequences, or sequel, to the story. Prophecy, however, is to be cautiously ventured upon, and no predictions should be pronounced with certainty as revealing predestination. Palmists can only foresee coming events when the factors of these exist in the individual character, or are set in motion by present influences, circumstances, and environment, but these laws being by no means immutable, there is always hope of escape from impending disaster. Favourable forecasts must not be looked upon either as infallible, otherwise disappointment may result.

A wise man will listen to the advice of the prophet, accept the encouragement it gives, and follow it only in so far as it accords with reason and good judgment. A happy forecast of a man's future will often start him on the right path, by putting into him a belief in himself and his own powers which he lacks, or has lost, and, by raising hope, courage, and perseverance, give him the stimulus necessary for the attainment of his desires. To take away hope, is to take away life. A doctor does not allow his patient to know the fears he has of his ultimate recovery, but tells him he will get well, and often to the amazement of the physician the sick man does recover. In the same way, to

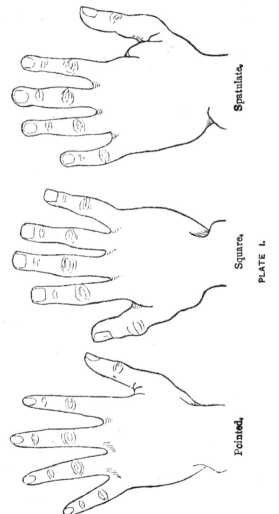

Pointed,

Square,

Spatulate,

PLATE I.

THE THREE TYPES OF HANDS.

fix the idea in a man's mind that he can and will succeed, goes a long way towards rendering him successful, and the palmist can point out the most favourable course to pursue, or the talents that will best repay cultivation.

And so in regard to other for s of prophecy the same maxim may be applied, justify a moderate practice of divination.

THE DIFFERENT TYPES.

For the sake of convenience, hands have been divided into three classes, although within these there are varieties, and absolutely pure types are seldom found. In most hands one type predominates, and we judge accordingly, allowing for modification through the class less indicated.

To discover the type we must look first at the back of the hands, noting the shape of the finger tips, which may be pointed, square or spatulate. (See Plate I., p. 5.) Conic is a combination that partakes of the qualities of spatulate and pointed. An intermediate type.

Pointed hands indicate thought or conception.

The "subject" has many ideas, but does not always put them into execution. He originates, and allows other people to carry out his suggestions.

Square hands show reasoning powers, enquiry, analysis, and not much ideality. They belong to people who take nothing on trust, but require every theory demonstrated, before their minds accept a new truth. They question and cross-examine, and are not receptive of inspirational or intuitive thought, and their minds are only reached through the conviction of the outward senses.

Spatulate hands belong to the workers of the world, or to those who love and lead an active life.

They like variety and change in their lives. Movement of every kind, and machinery in motion has a great fascination for them.

When we consider these significations we find that any pure type,—that is, all the fingers of one class, does not mark a desirable individual. All action and no thought—reason without inspiration—or ideas without the power of putting them into practice, would not make a useful or wise citizen of the world. We want a mixture of the three types to give the proper balance, and this we find in most people. One type, however, usually outweighs the others, and gives us the keynote of the character.

THE FINGERS AND PALM CONSIDERED.

Shortfingered people are not given to detail, they judge of the whole of things, and do not analyse. They are quick in forming their opinions, hasty, impulsive, and energetic in personal movement.

People with long fingers are slow in speech, action, and in coming to any decision. They are fond of detail, are inquisitive, often fidgety, and inclined to worry other people with their fastidiousness and love of order. The fingers and palm should be of equal length to form a well-balanced character. The palm should neither be too narrow nor too wide. It should be almost square, as broad across the upper part of the hand as at the base, which will show that the intellectual and material natures are equally developed and controlled.

The mounts under the fingers (see Plate II., p. 21) symbolise the intellectual and spiritual side of man,—the mounts across the lower part of the hand represent the passions, emotions, and animal tendencies.

THE KNOTS.

The developments of the finger joints are called **knots.** In the hands of some people the fingers are quite smooth, but in others the joints distort the outline and destroy the beauty of the hand. They have their value nevertheless. In the eyes of a chirologist, the **narrow, smooth, pointed hand** artists love to portray, is not beautiful—it speaks to him of **selfishness, laziness, uselessness,** an altogether unpractical nature. Although the owner may have exalted sentiments and high ideals, no work will be carried out unless there are some other strongly developed counteracting points in the character.

The first knot (counting from the nail downwards) is called the knot of **philosophy**—which questions, investigates, and reasons on abstract subjects. This knot when found only on the finger of **Jupiter** (the index or fore-finger) is an evidence of **scepticism,** or freedom of thought in religious matters. The owner will form a creed for himself, and will not be bound down by any dogma.

The second knot gives **order** and method in the management of business and affairs, punctuality and exactness.

The third knot (where the fingers join the hand) is considered by some chirologists, to indicate **order in household matters.**

The absence of knots denotes a **rapid influx of ideas.** In a talented hand the thoughts are spontaneous, inspiration and sentiment will guide and control, unchecked by reason or criticism. With smooth fingers a **religious enthusiast** will be carried away by devotion, and may become a **fanatic.**

The first knots being present on all the fingers and the second knots absent, will render the individual critical and fault-finding, but unpractical.

When the first and second knots are both in evidence, there is a tendency to investigation, analysis, and criticism. ⁕ The "subject" is thoroughly practical, methodical and logical. He delights in argument and does not readily concede a point.

A musician with knotted hand will play correctly, but mechanically and without feeling.

A painter with knotted fingers will understand the mixing of colours, his drawing will be correct, but there will be no inspiration in his work.

A man of letters with the same form of hand will exhibit little imagination in the writing of his books. Histories, biographies, travels will be more within his scope than poesy or imaginative plots and descriptions.

Square tipped and knotted fingers have a great leaning towards science, deduction and calculation.

Spatulate and knotted fingers are characterized by the love of locomotion, navigation, engineering and manual labour.

Pointed and knotted fingers are less prone to enthusiasm, romance and fancy than smooth pointed, and are more practical generally.

CHAPTER II

The Fingers and Palms

THE **fingers** are the principal index of the **talents** and capabilities. They are considered good when straight, well-developed, and in proportion to the rest of the hand. Their **bases** should be **nearly on a level**—this is one of the **signs of success**, or rather of the qualities that make for success. A finger set below the others loses much of its power.

JUPITER. SIGN ♃.

The **Index**, or fore-finger, when straight and of good length, indicates uprightness of character, a strong sense of justice and honour.

If it comes prominently forward, a desire to lead, or rule, is shown.

Should it fall behind the other fingers, a dislike to responsibility is indicated.

When short, there is not much feeling of duty or obligation.

The " subject " will be guided more by inclination, and will not sacrifice himself for others, or for any special object, such as patriotism, or devotion to his profession.

A crooked Jupiter finger denotes a lack of honour.

Too long a finger of Jupiter will make the "subject" domineering, and tyrannical if the thumb be long also.

A pointed Jupiter finger gives quick apprehension, intuition, and a love of reading.

Square. A love of truth, but bluntness of speech.

Spatulate. Dulness of perception.

SATURN. SIGN

By this name and sign the Medius, or middle finger is known.

When well-developed it gives to the nature seriousness, depth and balance.

If too long, extreme caution is shown. A man with this characteristic will miss his chances in life, fearing to take an important step lest he may run some risk.

A short finger of Saturn, on the contrary, will cause him to rush into dangers, as a want of prudence and calculation is thereby shown.

When this finger is crooked, the temperament is apprehensive and morbid.

A pointed Saturn finger is indicative of frivolity. No serious thought will be given to anything either worldly or spiritual.

A spatulate finger of Saturn shows activity, bodily or mental, according to the other signs the hand displays.

A square Saturn finger gives prudence. Its possessor will reason and calculate before coming to any decision, or before embarking on any enterprise; he will think deeply on all subjects, and the advice he gives will be first carefully considered; he never jumps to conclusions or acts upon impulse.

APOLLO. SIGN ☉

The Annularius, or ring-finger, styled **Apollo**, is the indicator of art and literature.

When too long, talents will be turned to the acquirement of wealth.

Speculation, the taste for gambling, or the love of games of chance, are seen when the finger is almost the same height as the middle finger.

Well-developed, the Apollo finger shows a literary or artistic nature, but this must be taken in conjunction with other signs.

With a good Head-line (see Plate III., p. 27) and pointed finger of Jupiter, the inclination will probably be towards literature.

When the Apollo finger comes prominently forward, art is more often indicated.

A crooked finger of Apollo shows that the talent is used more as a means of making money, than from devotion to the profession, or love of the presiding goddess.

A pointed Apollo finger indicates artistic feeling, but no practical art.

A spatulate Apollo gives a love of colour, dramatic talent, movement in art. Painters with this form of finger will depict animals, scenes with incident, and portraits.

With a square Apollo there is realism in art or literature.

MERCURY. SIGN ☿.

The Auricularis, or little finger, is so called.

A good Mercury finger is required for success generally—social and in business.

It should be straight, and on a level with the other fingers.

When it is set low on the hand there will be a great struggle against circumstances, and if these are to be overcome the finger must not be crooked.

A straight finger of Mercury gives the capacity for making use of talents and opportunities.

If long and prominent the " subject " will, without difficulty, make his way in the world, even to the surmounting of obstacles. It will be his nature to " walk over," or find a way round these—all the powers he possesses will be used in the endeavour.

When short, the above qualities are lacking.

A crooked finger shows a want of good management and diplomacy—chances will be missed, and the people who might be of use in the advancement of the career will be slighted or neglected. The "subject's" mental vision in this respect will not be clear or far-sighted.

A pointed Mercury finger denotes tact. With this shape of finger deficiencies in other qualities will be made up—the want of knowledge or talent will not be marked, for the "subject" will know how to veil his ignorance, and will quietly pick up information, and use the opportunities that offer.

In a spatulate Mercury finger good management of business and affairs is shown.

A square Mercury finger gives scientific reasoning and preceptive qualities.

THE POLLEX, OR THUMB.

Although last on the list, the thumb is the most important of all the fingers, as in it the indication of will-power lies.

A long, well-developed first phalange (see Plate II., p. 21) shows strength of purpose, constancy in friendship and affection. The second phalange being in proportion, the will is guided by reason.

A wide stretch between the first finger and thumb indicates a generous nature—when at the same time the first phalange turns back—extravagance, or the love of spending money. With a good Heart-line (see Plate III., p. 27) the "subject" will spend on others as well as on himself.

A thumb close to the hand, and stiff, denotes extreme care of money, but with a broad palm will not show meanness.

The turning back of the tip of the thumb is one

of the signs of dramatic talent, but this alone will not make an actor (see chapter on Professions and Trades).

The thumb should be large, but not too heavy, otherwise the "subject" will be obstinate and tyrannical. If too small, indecision of character is the result.

When set low down on the hand there is versatility, but taking up many things the "subject" is not likely to excel in any.

When the thumb is clubbed—that is, very heavy at the top and out of proportion to the rest of the finger, other signs being unfavourable—a brutal nature is shown.

A pointed thumb shows susceptibility to flattery and the influence of other people.

Spatulate. The owners of this form of thumb will be decided in their opinions, and hold to them obstinately, particularly when the first knot is developed.

When square, the will-power is controlled by reason.

THE PALM.

The relative length of the fingers and palm is first to be considered When these are equal good judgment is shown, and, other signs agreeing, advice from this person may be confidently acted upon.

A firm palm indicates an active, energetic nature.

A soft palm is the sign of laziness and self-indulgence.

A thick palm betrays a selfish and egotistical character.

A hollow palm shows a want of aggressiveness, a peace-loving disposition. When a man has to make his way in the world it is a drawback to have a hand hollow in the centre. He will, with this sign, allow other people to push him aside, and will not fight against adverse circumstances. In home life he will often give way simply for the sake of peace, even when in the right, and although this implies amiability, it also shows a defective character.

A **wide palm** denotes tolerance and generosity of mind. When it is firm at the same time, a love of open-air life and occupations is shown.

A **narrow palm** signifies meanness, and a want of sympathy and consideration for others.

A **flat palm** shows a certain amount of combativeness. The owner can stand up for himself, and will hold his own against the world.

A **much-lined palm** is an indication of a nervous temperament and sensitive nature.

CHAPTER III

The Nails and Phalanges

THE NAILS. INDICATIONS OF TEMPER.

THE nails chiefly indicate the temper of the subject, but must not be taken as the sole guide. The Mount of Mars (see Plate II., p. 21), should be examined to ascertain the amount of self-control the owner possesses. The thumb also must be looked at, as it shows the strength of will, and how far the subject is able to subdue his feelings of anger, or whether passion will overcome him. We must also inspect the lines, as illnesses of all kinds, and particularly of the nerves, have a great effect upon the temper, making a naturally sweet disposition irritable and peevish.

The hardships and anxieties of life must also be taken into account, for mental worry will often make a person appear impatient or morose.

Filbert-shaped nails of pale pink colouring show a sweet temper. The same shape, but red, a hasty temper—anger, however, is not lasting. Filbert shaped white nails, those who are not easily roused to anger, but when displeased do not readily forget.

Short red nails indicate an irritable and passionate disposition.

Short nails, square at the base, with a high plain of Mars (the space between the two mounts) (see Plate II., p. 21), mark the person as pugnacious, he will be the first to pick a quarrel. Possessors of short round nails are critical, irritable, but not passionate. Short, round and very white nails show a cynical nature. Large white, square nails mark one that is revengeful, that will wait its opportunity, but will not forget. Nails pointed at the base show a disposition that is easily offended, and quick to fancy slights.

A short nail on the finger of Mercury indicates mockery, and with other signs the power of mimicry. These people are very quick to see oddities and idiosyncrasies in others.

Large nails usually accompany good business qualities.

Very bright nails indicate quick mental apprehension. But care must be taken to distinguish between nails that have been manicured and those that are naturally bright.

THE NAILS AS INDICATORS OF HEALTH.

With hard nails we see a tendency to paralysis. Fluted nails show a tendency to rheumatism, acne, eczema, and other skin diseases. White spots on nails indicate a derangement of the digestive organs. Very thin nails are indicative of general delicacy. High curved nails are among the signs of consumption. Dents on the nails indicate past illnesses.

With small half moons, or when these are over developed, there is evidence of bad circulation.

THE PHALANGES.

The phalanges are the three divisions on each finger (see Plate II., p. 21), the first being that which contains the nail. Desbarolles makes these representative of the three worlds. The first signifying the spiritual or psychic, the second, the intellectual world; the third, the material. In pursuance of this theory, the first phalanges of all the fingers being well developed, the aspirations are exalted. Good second phalanges, give intellectual tastes. The third phalanges of all the fingers, thick and long, show a love of eating and drinking, and indulgence in material pleasures. Each finger must, however, be taken separately, and the phalanges thereon considered by themselves.

JUPITER.

A long first phalange on this finger indicates religious feeling, or more broadly speaking, psychological tendencies—for the word religion embraces much more than church attendance, the observance of forms and ceremonies, and adherence to certain creeds. The second phalange is that of ambition—self-advancement. The third phalange long gives the love of ruling. Short phalanges show the want of the above characteristics.

SATURN.

The first phalange long denotes a leaning towards melancholy sentiments. A sadness in the temperament. The second phalange of Saturn long, shows a love of agriculture, gardening and so forth. A long third phalange gives economy.

APOLLO.

The first phalange long. A love of art and beauty.

The second phalange long. An intellectual appreciation of art. Artists with this characteristic will not only paint, but will study the history and development of art, and the lives of the great masters.

The third phalange of Apollo when long shows a love of riches, fondness for display, and personal vanity.

MERCURY.

First phalange long. Eloquence in speech is indicated. If in excess, it reveals a capacity for lying.

The second phalange long denotes a love of science or scientific pursuits.

A long third phalange on this finger gives diplomacy. When in excess the "subject" is unscrupulous and given to scheming.

PHALANGES OF THE THUMB.

The first phalange long shows constancy, firmness of character and strength of will. When too long, a despotic nature. If short, indecision of character, a variable will.

The second phalange, if properly developed, gives reasoning and logical powers. When "waisted," that is, falling in at the sides, there will be little capacity for argument, or for looking at both sides of a question.

The third phalange shows the emotional nature. When it is over-developed, the subject will be governed by passion. When properly proportioned it denotes a love of humanity. On the angles of this phalange music is shown. The upper angle gives time. The lower angle, tune (see Plate IV., Frontispiece). On the Mount of Venus (the fleshy part of this phalange, see Plate II., p. 21), the love of melody is to be found. The power of execution is seen in the flexibility of the fingers, and composition, when the finger tips in a musical hand are square.

CHAPTER IV

The Mounts and their Attributes

IMMEDIATELY under the third phalanges of the fingers are to be found little mounds or risings which take the names of the fingers above them. There are others on the lower part of the hand, namely—the two Mounts of Mars which lie beneath the mounts of Jupiter and Mercury (see Plate II., p. 21), divided from the former by the Life-line, and from the latter by the Line of Heart (see Plate III., p. 27). The Plain of Mars separates the two mounts of that name. Luna is placed under Mars on the percussion, or outside of the hand, and opposite to it, on the third phalange of the thumb is Venus. The mounts are sometimes displaced and encroach upon each other, in which case they are influenced by the qualities of the mount towards which they lean. They are also sometimes absent from the hand, this signifies a lack of the virtue represented by the mount.

Over-developed mounts are unfavourable, as showing faults of character, the result of good qualities becoming perverted, or carried to excess. Proper pride is desirable, but too much pride renders the person overbearing and imperious. Courage is a good trait, but too much of it makes a man foolhardy. Imagination may lead to folly, wit and merriment to buffoonery, and so on.

The mounts are considered good when they are well-placed, evenly developed, and firm to the touch. The upper and lower mounts should be proportionately developed. When the upper are more in

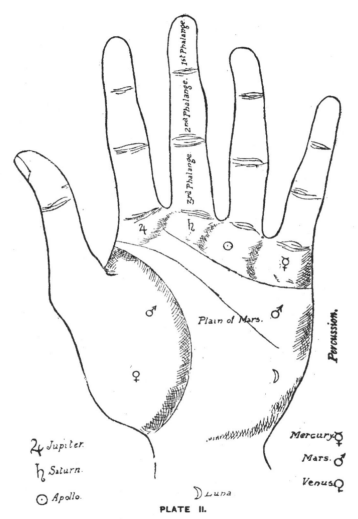

PLATE II.

THE MOUNTS AND PHALANGES.

evidence, the intellectual qualities will prevail over the animal tendencies, but if the lower are more developed, the passions have the supremacy. When all are apparently absent, an unemotional nature is shown ; but in reality it will be found that they are so evenly developed as to make the hand appear flat. This will not signify an entire want of feeling, only that the emotions are well under control. It is more frequently observable in a man's hand, he having been taught in his school-boy days that any display of feeling is considered unmanly, and later, in contact with the world, that it is not judicious to allow sentiment to influence the life.

A woman's hand as a rule shows more "hills." But the training of the present day girl will do much to flatten these, as the system now in vogue tends to harden the nature, and make sentiment give place to practical common sense. So the "New Woman" may in the future, as far as her hand is concerned, attain her ambition—equality with man.

THE MOUNT OF JUPITER. ♃

This mount when well developed shows a love of society and family. Self-respect and proper pride. In excess it manifests haughtiness and conceit. If absent selfishness, and a want of self-respect is revealed.

THE MOUNT OF SATURN. ♄

When well-developed this mount gives to the character gravity and caution, and evinces a love of solitude. In excess morbidness, fear and mania. Absent, extreme melancholy will be a prominent note in the nature of the "subject."

THE MOUNT OF APOLLO. ☉

A well developed mount of **Apollo** endows the character with the quality of mercy, with a love of beauty and art, and gives a desire for fame. In excess, vanity, ostentation, a love of money, or notoriety. When absent cruelty will form a feature of the character.

THE MOUNT OF MERCURY. ☿

If this mount is well developed there is general buoyancy and spirit. It gives hope, wit, merriment, and great recuperative power. The "subject" endowed with the qualities of this mount will rise above troubles and adversity, and make light of his ailments. In excess, the mount shows ruse and scheming. If absent, there is no sense of humour.

THE MOUNT OF MARS. ♂ (*Under Jupiter*).

This mount when well developed shows moral courage, self-control, the power of forgiveness. In excess, reserve, great strength of resistance. If absent there is no power of endurance.

THE MOUNT OF MARS. ♂ (*Under Mercury*).

When this mount is "good," it gives active, aggressive courage, promptitude, and a love of danger. It is essentially the soldiers' mount, without it a man will not go to the front from choice. In excess, it shows rashness and daring. If absent, there is a want of courage and presence of mind.

THE MOUNT OF LUNA. ☽

Well developed, this mount displays imagination, sentiment, sympathy, and gives a love of beautiful scenery. In excess, folly, caprice and eccentricity. Absent, discontent, and a want of sympathy and imagination.

THE MOUNT OF VENUS. ♀

With this mount well developed the nature is benevolent, affectionate and demonstrative. It gives also a love of melody and the pleasures of the senses. In excess, sensuality. When absent there is coldness and selfishness in the disposition.

THE MOUNTS DISPLACED.

The deviation of the mounts from their proper places denotes various qualities or characteristics, according to the direction taken, thus:—Should Jupiter encroach upon Saturn, self-consciousness will be the result. Saturn encroaching on Apollo gives sadness in art. Apollo inclining to Mercury, shows a love of children and animals, with gentleness and mercy. With Mercury joined to Mars, there is courage in emergency. Mars rising to Mercury, courage of opinions. When Luna sinks towards the Bracelet, the " subject " is given to day dreams—to "building castles in the air." **Venus** encroaching on the Bracelet shows a love of dancing. **Note.** The **Rascettes** or **Bracelets** are the lines that encircle the **wrist** (see Plate IV. Frontispiece).

THE COMBINATION OF MOUNTS.

The two most prominent mounts in the hand have next to be considered, as this will also give an indication of certain qualities or properties.

Jupiter and Mercury together, make a worldly person, loving society and entertainment.

With Jupiter and Apollo, justice and mercy go hand in hand; these people make good rulers.

Jupiter and Venus. Persons with this combination like to shine in society, and are fond of admiration.

Saturn and Mercury, will be lively in company, but dull and gloomy when alone.

Saturn and Mars, prudent and calculating.

Saturn and Luna, are apprehensive. This combination gives tragedy in art.

With Apollo and Luna there is great imagination in art or literature.

Apollo and Mars in an artistic hand incline the owner to select battle scenes for the subjects of his pictures, will make a war correspondent, etc. Mercury and Mars: These people love practical jokes. Mercury and Venus: Together these mounts form the flirt, or make the " subject " gay and good-humoured. Mercury and Luna, in an actor's hand will make him a comedian, or an artist, a caricaturist. Venus and Apollo give kindliness and the love of humanity, and will make the philanthropist.

When the Mount of Saturn is much developed and Jupiter absent, there is a hatred of society, or of one's own family.

When Jupiter and Luna are present, but Mercury lacking, wonderful projects are conceived, but not put into execution.

These examples will suffice, although numerous combinations may be worked out. In those presented, it is to be noted that the favourable qualities of the mounts are taken, presuming that they are what is called " well developed." The combination of mounts " in excess," as the reader will readily understand, would produce totally different characters.

CHAPTER V

On the Principal Lines

COMING now to the most interesting but intricate part of Palmistry, let me first lay before the reader some well-founded explanation of the markings and lines found more or less on every hand. Many people imagine that these are caused by hard work, quite the reverse is the case, however.

The hand of a labourer, or other manual worker, as a rule is devoid of lines, with the exception of the three or four principal ones which very few hands are without, namely, the Life, Head, Heart and Fate Lines (see Plate III., p. 27), while a lady of means and position, who has no necessity for soiling her fingers, or who has no inclination for active employment or amusements, will frequently be found to have her palms covered with a network of fine lines, that is, if she be of a highly nervous temperament.

Work, sport and active games of all kinds steady the nerves, distract the thoughts from self, and instead of making lines, they smooth out those that have previously appeared, and prevent the formation of others.

It is the feelings affecting the brain that act upon the hand, and leave there the record of what the "subject" has gone through, either in reality or in imagination and morbid apprehension. Events and experiences that are not deeply felt—even though tragic—may leave no impression, if the person be of a philosophic or phlegmatic nature, or one who easily forgets.

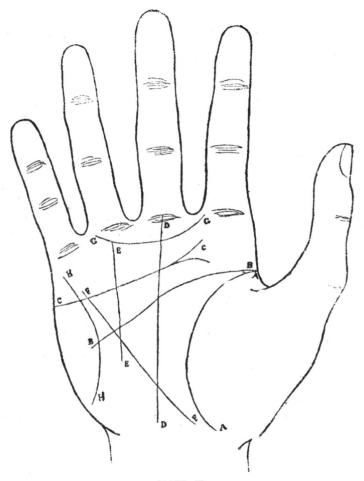

PLATE III.

The Principal Lines.

A—A. The Life Line.	E—E. The Line of Apollo.
B—B. The Head Line.	F—F. The Hepatica.
C—C. The Heart Line.	G—G. The Ring of Saturn.
D—D. The Fate Line.	H—H. The Line of Intuition.

I have examined the hands of a sailor who was twice shipwrecked, but could find no sign of the disaster, the explanation being that—to use his own words—he " considered it rather a lark." He was of a sanguine, careless disposition, and on both occasions was within sight of land.

This is one of the difficulties of Palmistry—to discriminate between the real experiences, and the nervous fancies of a sensitive nature. When we find a hand very much crossed with fine hair lines we must always allow a wide margin for extreme sensitiveness, and imagination in regard to troubles.

My experience is that the markings on the hand are more indicative of sorrows and cares than of joys. Pleasures do not stamp either the face or hand in the same degree as misfortunes and calamities. It may not be inappropriate here to state that post-mortem examination of the hands of the blind has disclosed the fact that, in the nerves at the end of the fingers, cells of grey matter had formed identical in substance with the grey matter of the brain, by which no doubt the lack of vision was supplied, the extreme sensitiveness of touch enabling the man deprived of sight to " sense " what he cannot see, indicating a close connection between the hand and brain.

A theory might be built upon this fact to account for the reflection on the palms of thoughts that agitate the brain, or experiences that have left an impression on the mind. Certainly the smaller lines are not mere " creases." Whether those of Head, Heart or Life may be due to the folding of the hand is still an unsettled question, some Palmists maintaining that it is so. But, as these lines take so many different courses, become blurred or disappear, this suggestion is at least doubtful.

THE PRINCIPAL LINES.

The four most important lines are :—**The Line of Life, The Fate Line, The Head Line, and The Line of Heart** (see Plate III., p. 27). The two latter sometimes run together, appearing as one line, but they are both there nevertheless, and the joining of the two has a special significance. The minor lines are subject to greater changes of position, and are frequently not to be found at all. A much-lined hand indicates a nervous temperament or impressionable nature.

The hands of women generally display **more lines** than do those of **men**, their nerves being weaker, and feelings naturally more acute, or less blunted by contact with the world. The hand of a person who has no susceptibility or depth of feeling, whether man or woman, will show very few lines.

The lines are not stationary, they **grow, alter, fade** and **reappear.** Such being the case, it is **not possible to foretell** accurately the number of years that may be allotted to the "subject," nor with **certainty** any coming event, although many predictions deduced from indications found on the hand do fulfil themselves. There is comfort to be derived from this also, that even when the liability **to disease or disaster** is there, the fatality **may be avoided.** Palmistry does not pronounce an unalterable decree. We only claim that the science erects the **sign-post to direct or warn,** so that we may escape the evils that threaten.

THE LINE OF LIFE.

This line commences under the finger of **Jupiter,** and encircles the Mount of Venus. In the left hand it shows the inherited constitution of the " subject."

In the right hand are seen on it the illnesses gone through, and those that may occur.

Both hands must be carefully compared before a warning is given of coming sickness, or liability to any disease. The Life-line should be long, clear and unbroken. This will denote a long life and freedom from illness. A break in the line indicates an illness, or great debility of health—if in both hands, it is accentuated. However, should this sign be present, there is still no certainty of a breakdown, for if care be taken during the period of life where the break occurs, the line will mend, or a double line appear as the danger passes.

A short Life-line is not always a sign of early decease, but shows that caution is necessary at the age where the line ends (see Plate VIII., p. 53, Measurement of Time). If the constitution is built up again the line will grow.

The clearest sign of departure from this life is the stopping of all the principal lines at the same date, even then there may be preservation marks (see Plate VII., p. 49), and it is wiser in reading hands never to pronounce judgment on this point, as in nervous individuals the prophecy may have the effect of bringing about its own fulfilment.

A double Life-line will give strength of constitution, and a high Mount of Mercury recuperative power, the spirits and natural buoyancy having great influence over the physical health.

Small lines crossing the Life-line indicate family troubles, or illnesses. A chained Life-line is the sign of a long period of ill-health. When the Life-line ends in a fork there is great loss of vitality. Ending in a star or cross (see Plate VII., p. 49), it denotes sudden death, or accident. When the Life-line sends down a branch towards Luna death in a foreign land, or a long residence abroad, is foreshadowed. Islands, dots, circles, and other marks on this line show different maladies, and are dealt with in another chapter.

THE HEAD LINE.

The Head-line usually begins with the Life-line, crossing the hand towards the Mount of Luna. By this line the intellectual capacity is judged.

A long sloping Head-line will give mental activity and imagination, but not necessarily intelligence. A deep Head-line shows greater powers of concentration. If short and deep, concentration on certain subjects only.

When the Head-line slopes too much on to the Mount of Luna eccentricity will be the result.

A short straight Head-line gives practical common sense and good business qualities. When long and straight the acquisition of money will be the motive power of the " subject's " life.

A double Head-line denotes an interest in some study or pursuit apart from the career.

A forked Head-line (see Plate VII., p. 49), shows diplomacy, a tendency to exaggerate or veil the truth, and with a long finger of Mercury, the capacity for deliberate lying.

The Head-line joined to the Life-line for some distance towards the middle of the hand is indicative of slow development of mind and lack of self-confidence.

These two lines, wide apart in both hands, show independence, rashness, and audacity. In the right hand only, self-reliance has been acquired. In the left only, independence has been repressed.

It is not a good sign when the Head and Heart-lines are joined as if one line. It shows some physical weakness of the heart or brain, and also a struggle between desire and judgment. This unfavourable aspect of these lines is frequently found in the hands of people of great intelligence, seldom in those of a small-minded person, and therefore would seem to indicate a greater strain upon the mental powers than the corporal strength of the organ is able to endure. An islanded Head-line shows weakness from over-study, or illness in which delirium has occurred. When the line of Head is chained there is a want of stability in the ideas. The Head-line stopping at the Fate-line shows an unlucky, troubled life or arrested development. A feathered Head-line (see Plate VII., p. 49) is the indication of a strain upon the brain, liability to a nervous break-down.

THE HEART LINE.

This line rises under the Mount of Mercury and ascends towards or on to the Mount of Jupiter. The capacity for affection is measured by this line. It is also an indicator of the state of the heart itself. It should be narrow, clear, long, and branched. Placed low down on the hand, it will give high aspirations and ideals. When it lies close to the fingers it shows a jealous and exacting nature. When long the Heart-line signifies a loving disposition. Rising up between the fingers of Jupiter and Saturn, too much feeling and devotion. The "subject" will sacrifice himself to his affections or work. Terminating on the Mount of Jupiter, ideal love is shown, but when the line goes right round the percussion of this mount, there is an intensity of passion which may lead to crime. A short Heart-line indicates selfishness.

Branches from the Heart-line denote friendships; when these are crossed disappointment in friends. A Heart-line without branches shows a loveless, isolated life. A branch from the Heart-line dropping on to the Life-line is the sign of a loss, probably through death, of a much-loved friend.

A forked Heart-line is desirable, as it is an indication of trustworthiness and affection.

A double Heart-line is seldom found unless the physical organ is weak or has sustained injury, in which case it will show recuperative power enabling the person to survive the shock or outgrow the malady.

When the Heart and Head-lines are placed close to one another, the "subject" is narrow-minded or engrossed with his own affairs; but if the space widen towards Mars (under Mercury) his ideals and interests are capable of development.

The absence of a Heart-line shows a hardened nature, but the individual is generally successful through selfishness and want of consideration for others. The signs of illness to be found on the Heart-line are described in the chapter on Diseases and Maladies.

THE LINE OF FATE.

On the Fate-line we read the events of life, changes, successes or failures, and the possibilities of the future.

The starting-point of the Fate-line varies very much. It may rise from the Rascettes (see Plate IV., Frontispiece), from the Life-line, from Luna, or from the plain of Mars (see Plate II., p. 21). It is sometimes entirely absent, which, if in both hands, will show a very uneventful life.

When the Fate-line rises from Luna and makes

for Saturn, the strong influence of another person over the life is indicated. In a woman's hand this is sometimes a sign of marriage, but she will be much under the control of her partner. In the right hand, the Fate-line taking this direction shows material help or advancement.

The Fate-line starting on Luna, and travelling towards Jupiter, is a good sign, and indicates an improvement in social position, due to some one outside of the family circle.

When the Fate-line proper stops, and a branch rises, it shows a change of career, and the direction of the branch must be observed, as it will point out the probable consequence of the change according to the direction the branch takes.

When the Fate-line rises from the Life-line the "subject" has not broken away from his family, or should he have left home, his interests are still with his own people.

When the Fate-line starts right away from the Life-line an independent career is denoted or early responsibility.

The Fate-line beginning on the Mount of Mars is the sign of success late in life, after a prolonged struggle with circumstances.

A waving Line of Fate shows uncertainty concerning the career. With a line of this kind a man will do nothing great, and will probably spoil his life by want of stability or lack of judgment.

Breaks on the Fate-line mark important changes in the life.

Lines running across the Fate-line represent obstacles in the path, or when they come from within the Life-line, the deaths of relatives.

The doubling of the Fate-line is always a good sign. It denotes improvement of position. When

the "sister" or secondary line lies close to the
Fate-line proper, it will improve the surroundings
without altering the life, when at a distance, and a
break occurs at the same time, the destiny will be
changed.

A chained Fate-line indicates a troubled life.
When it stops at the Head-line an error of
judgment adversely affects the career.

Branches falling downwards from the Fate-line
show reverses. Branches rising upwards, enter-
prises or new interests in life; if uncrossed they are
likely to be successful.

If the Fate-line itself or a branch therefrom seeks
the Mount of Jupiter, ambition is gratified or
social position attained. Should the course of the
branch or line be towards Saturn, an ordinary
career is indicated.

When the line makes for the Mount of Apollo,
riches or fame will be the lot of that individual.

Going in the direction of Mercury, the Fate-line
promises success in commercial undertakings or in
scientific pursuits.

The events and illnesses seen on the Life-line
should be corroborated on the Line of Fate.

CHAPTER VI

Fortune, Health, Marriage, and other Lines

THE LINE OF APOLLO

THE line of Fortune, or Apollo-line (see Plate III., p. 27), shows, not so much the state of the finances as the extent to which money matters exercise the mind, whether in anxiety over these or in the acquisition of riches.

A clear uncrossed line is indicative of wealth or comfortable circumstances, due to freedom from care in respect of money.

The Apollo-line runs upwards under the finger of Apollo, and may start from the Life-line, the plain of Mars, from the Mount of Luna, or from the Head-line.

When there are two or more deeply marked lines of Apollo, it denotes money from more than one source.

A broken Apollo-line, or with bars across, shows loss of money. In the left hand, family loss; in the right, personal.

Lines rising from within the Life-line and cutting through or breaking the Apollo-line, are signs of money losses through relatives; if, on the contrary they join, or run alongside of it, they point to the inheritance of money.

A long line from Venus to the Apollo line shows inherited property or wealth. Lines in the same manner from Mars or Mercury joining, or doubling the Apollo-line, indicate money received from other people, not necessarily by legacy—they may be gifts, compensation, or reward of some kind. Should these lines cut through or break the Apollo line, loss of money by treachery, mismanagement, or theft is shown.

Lines from Luna joining the Apollo-line represent legacies.

When the Apollo-line rises from the Head-line success will only come late in life. Rising from the plain of Mars (see Plate II., p. 21), it indicates a struggle in the race for wealth. **Rising from Luna** it shows fortune gained by the help or influence of other people, or **by Marriage**.

Lines from the Apollo-line show to some extent in what manner money has been, or is to be made. If these lines point towards Mercury, it will be attained in business or commercial enterprise. If towards Saturn, by investment in land, property or mines.

If the Apollo-line itself rises steadily in the direction of the Mount, money will probably come through success n the profession or calling.

Transverse lines cutting the line of Apollo show **obstacles** in the way of success or money-making.

A line from the Fate-line to the line of Apollo **indicates business partnership.**

A number of small perpendicular lines on the Mount of Apollo indicate diversity of talents or tastes, none of which are likely to attain success, as it shows a want of concentration upon one study.

THE HEPATICA—OR LINE OF HEALTH.

The **absence** of this line indicates a **strong constitution**. When present, it should be long, narrow, straight and clear. It shows the state of the digestive organs, and general health.

The Hepatica (see Plate III., p. 27), should start from the Bracelets, or from the Line of Life, and rise towards Mercury. It is very erratic, however, and may be found elsewhere.

If tortuous or uneven, this line shows a tendency to biliousness. When broken, digestion is impaired; if very red, there is liability to fever; white and broad, it shows chronic dyspepsia. Small lines cutting through the Hepatica indicate bilious headaches. Islands on this line are always a bad sign, and point to internal ailments, sometimes indicating operations.

THE LINE OF INTUITION—(see Plate III., p.27).

This line rises on the Mount of Luna, and curves round to the Mount of Mercury. It is only found on the hands of persons who are gifted with intuitive faculties. If seen in both hands, these are inherited and developed. If in the left hand only, the power is inherited, but latent.

With this line deeply marked, a pointed finger of Jupiter, and high Mount of Luna, the " subject " should be highly sensitive to occult influences. An island on this Line is said to show the gift of clairvoyance, or " second sight."

THE RING OF SATURN.

Although not possessing the malignant properties attributed to it by some authors, who name it the " Girdle of Venus," the Ring of Saturn (see Plate III., p. 27), is not a favourable sign. Cutting, as it does, through the lines of Fate and Fortune, shutting out the benign influence of Apollo's Mount, and the prudence and wisdom derived from Saturn, it cannot be otherwise than hurtful. It is usually taken as a sign of misfortune in regard to love or friendship, but it is just as often the indication of disappointment in the career. When the line is broken or tangled, the failure of desires or ambitions is accentuated, and in this form it is a sign of nervous excitability and hysteria.

When the Ring of Saturn extends as far as the Influence lines on Mercury (see Plate IV., Frontispiece), and particularly if it join one of them, unhappiness and disappointment in love may with certainty be read.

MINOR LINES.

Among the Minor Lines, those dealing with matrimony will, to most people, be of the greatest interest, so we will take them first. These are to be seen rising from Luna towards the Fate-line (see Plate IV., Frontispiece). Lines within the Life-line taking their departure from this line towards Venus (see Plate IV., Frontispiece), and horizontal lines on the Mount of Mercury (see Plate IV., Frontispiece), are also indicative of love or marriage. Properly speaking, these are all called Influence-lines, and there is no distinct sign in itself which reveals or promises marriage.

It is difficult to determine with certainty either that the ceremony has been, or will be performed. Accuracy of reading will only come with experience, and perhaps intuition, but the following indications will serve for guidance in the settling of this most important question :—

First. When the Line from Luna touches the Fate-line without cutting it, and is clear and uncrossed.

Second. When the Line on the Mount of Mercury is neither crossed, forked, or otherwise marred.

Third. When the Influence-line within the Life-line has the same favourable aspect.

Fourth. When these lines are seen in both hands and in addition a well-formed cross (see Plate V., p. 41), appears on the Mount of Jupiter.

All these signs being present, it is quite safe to make the statement, but it frequently happens that, lacking this confirmation, marriage has taken place, so the-Palmist must proceed cautiously.

Should none of these signs be found on a hand, it is almost as certain that no marriage has occurred, and that no influence has entered the life. It is not an indication, however, of a life of celibacy, as the lines grow, and time and opportunity may alter the hand. The Palmist can only say in such a case: "There is no sign at present of marriage."

When the Luna Influence-line stops short of the Fate line, and the "subject" has passed that age, the attachment has not come to anything. If the

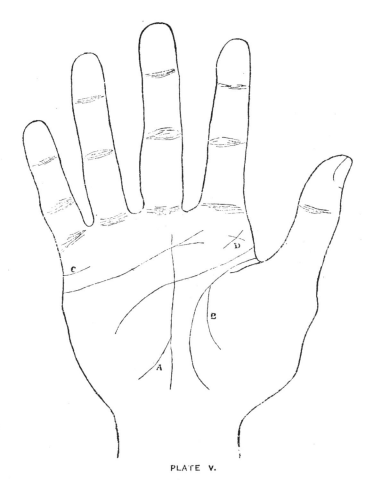

PLATE V.

SIGNS OF MARRIAGE.

A. Influence Line joining Fate Line without cutting it.
B. Influence Line Starting from Life Line and Traversing the Mount of Venus.
C. Mercury Influence Line Uncrossed.
D. Sign of Happy Marriage or Gratified Ambition.

age is not reached, then there is hope that the line may touch, and the love affair may end in marriage.

If it cut through the Fate-line, the engagement has been, or is likely to be, broken off, according to the date at which it crosses.

Small lines, barring the Influence-line, show interference or obstacles in the way of marriage.

When the Influence-line is islanded (see Plate VI., p. 45), it signifies ill-health or bad character of the fiancé or lover, and may prevent the marriage.

When the line is forked, it is also an unfavourable sign, and usually refers to health.

The Influence-lines on Mercury being forked, barred, or islanded—unhappy attachments, disappointed affection, and other love troubles are shown.

When the Mercury Influence-line drops on to the Heart-line (see Plate VI., p. 45), it is an indication of widowhood.

When it cuts the Heart-line and crosses over to Venus, or when a line rises from Venus, and makes for the Influence-line on Mercury (see Plate IV., Frontispiece), it is the sign of divorce or separation.

If the Influence-line within the Life-line is crossed, islanded, or forked, it will confirm the reading of the other signs. But none of these should be taken by itself, and it is only after careful comparison that the Palmist can arrive at a correct deduction.

If the Luna Influence-line is only to be found on the left hand, marriage will be uncertain, but desired. If on the right hand only, it will probably take place, but will not be a "love match," or at least, there will be more affection on the other side.

Sometimes the Luna Influence-line breaks and proceeds again towards the Fate-line. This will indicate anxieties connected with the engagement—breaks in the intimacy, and renewal of the connection; it may also indicate that the engaged couple have been parted by one or other taking a journey.

When these Influence-lines are long, they represent attachment to a friend of long standing. If short, the attraction of a new acquaintance.

Starting from Luna, on the percussion of the hand, they signify the influence of some person who is, or has been, abroad.

A star on any of these Influence-lines will show a great shock connected with the person, probably the death of the loved one (see Plate XIV., p. 99).

Marriages which take place late in life are more often shown by a break and change in the Fate-line than by Influence-lines, as these unions are usually more a matter of convenience, and have less romance than early attachments, but they are sometimes indicated in the same manner.

A line rising from the base of the thumb crossing to the Fate-line, signifies a step-father or mother, or guardian other than the natural parent.

All oblique lines touching the Fate-line from either side show the influence of other people over the life or career of the "subject." On the Luna side they are mostly of the opposite sex; from the Life-line it may be the influence of a friend of the same sex, or a member of the family.

VOYAGE LINES.

These are seen on the Mount of Luna. Rising from the Rascettes in the direction of Mars, long voyages are indicated.

Crossing the Mount horizontally, they indicate **shorter travels** and railway journeys. When clear and deeply marked they are pleasant; but when crossed, broken, or islanded, there is **danger** attached to them. A square (see Plate VII., p. 49) in close proximity shows **preservation** therefrom.

If marked on the left hand only, they are journeys contemplated, but not undertaken.

A **net-work of** lines on Luna shows a **nervous** temperament and tendency to neuralgia and disorders of the nerves.

ENMITY LINES (see Plate IV., Frontispiece).

Transverse lines on the Mount of Mars (under Mercury) are so called. The **power to do harm** will be shown if they touch or cross the Fate-line.

When these lines are islanded they denote **scandal** and evil speaking.

CHILDREN.

Perpendicular lines on the Mount of Mercury on the percussion of the hand are said to represent children, and from the appearance of the lines the sex and healthiness, or otherwise, of the offspring may be gathered.

Straight lines denote **boys**, slanting lines represent **girls**. If these lines are forked, or ill-formed, early death or delicacy in childhood is probable.

Stars, crosses, squares, etc., on these lines have much the same significance as on other lines. When the line runs up to the finger of Mercury, the child is likely to have a successful career.

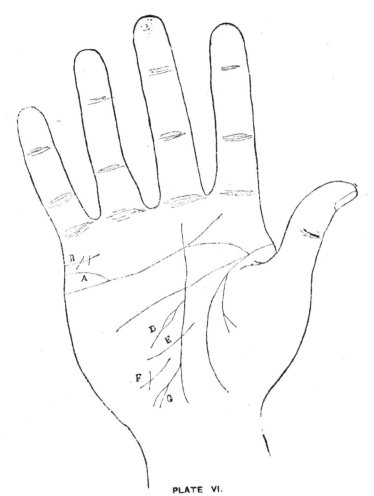

PLATE VI.

SIGNS OF WIDOWHOOD. DISAPPOINTED AFFECTION AND LOSS.

A. Widowhood.
A. Widowhood.
B. Disappointed Affection.
C. Loss through Death.

D. Obstacle in the way of Marriage, or obstacle to Marriage.
E. Broken Engagement.
F. Marriage Prevented.
G. Disappointment in regard to Marriage.

AMBITION LINES.

These rise from the Life-line towards the finger of Jupiter. If clear and uncrossed, gratified ambition is indicated. If barred, disappointment of some great desire.

A deep line on the first phalange of Jupiter shows ambition for, or deep interest in, some child.

THE LINE OF INTEMPERANCE

This line runs across the lower part of the hand from Luna to Venus. In the left hand only it will signify inherited tendency to intemperance. The "subject" having this sign should be advised to exercise caution in the use of stimulants.

When the line appears in the right hand only, he has probably suffered through the intemperance of some other person—a relative, or close connection.

If this line is found deeply marked in both hands, the thumb weak, and the hand generally shows lack of principle and self-control, it is safe to conclude that the "subject" indulges too freely in intoxicants; but the above signs must be unmistakable before such a deduction is drawn.

When the line of Intemperance is islanded, death from intoxication may ensue.

THE BRACELETS.

The Rascettes, or Bracelets, are the lines that encircle the wrist (see Plate IV., Frontispiece), but are not much taken into account by up-to-date Palmists. They are supposed to show the length of life; this, however, is more clearly indicated by the Lines of

Life and Fate. If the Rascettes rise towards the hand, it is a sign of noble thoughts and high aspirations; if they descend, the ambitions and desires are mundane.

A chained Rascette shows a life of hardship and work.

It is impossible to enumerate and describe every line that can be found upon the hand, as these vary in different people, coming and going in a few days, and have often no more significance than a passing worry.

By closely tracing the source and following the course of a line, the reader, from the hints already given, may find out for himself the cause of its appearance.

The Quadrangle is the space between the Head and Heart-lines in the centre of the hand.

The Triangle is formed by the junction of the Life-line, Head-line, and Hepatica.

CHAPTER VII

Stars, Crosses, and other Marks

HOW TO CALCULATE AGE AND TIME.

Stars on the hand are in no case of good omen. They signify fatalities, shocks, or disasters. They are the special danger signals of Palmistry.

Crosses, if well formed and clear, are occasionally favourable. These may appear on any part of the hand, and according to the place on which the mark is found the meaning of it is supplied.

STARS.

A star on the Mount of Jupiter signifies family trouble.

On the Mount of Saturn, it renders the person liable to accidents or misfortune.

On the Mount of Apollo, a loss of money is indicated; or celebrity won by chance, but not lasting.

On the Mount of Mercury, it shows loss by theft or treachery, dishonour in someone closely connected with the "subject."

On the Mount of Mars (under Mercury), the danger of being killed in battle, assassination, or murder.

On the Mount of Mars (under Jupiter) and near the Mount of Venus, a star shows legal proceedings.

On the Plain of Mars a star indicates railway accidents; also injury or loss through earthquakes.

On the Mount of Luna, it is a sign of illness, or if on a Voyage-line, the danger of drowning.

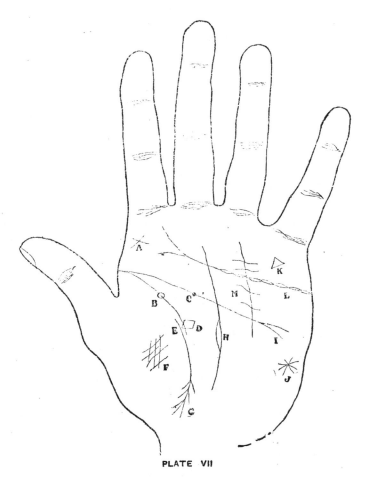

PLATE VII

SIGNS AND MARKS

A.	Cross.	**F.**	Grille.	**J.**	Star.
B.	Circle.	**G.**	Feathered Line.	**K.**	Triangle
C.	Dot or Spot.	**H.**	Island.	**L.**	Chained Line.
D.	Square (Preservation Mark).	**I.**	Fork.	**M.**	Barred Line.
E.	Break in The Life Line.				

On the Mount of Venus, trouble caused by love, or disappointment in marriage. If it appear on a line on this Mount, danger or misfortune to a friend or relative is denoted.

A star on the Life-line denotes death by accident, particularly if in both hands.

On the Head-line, trouble or shock, affecting the brain.

On the Heart-line, blindness through accident.

On the Apollo-line, a catastrophe. Great loss of money.

On the Quadrangle. When a star is seen here the " subject " is likely to be deceived by a friend.

On the Triangle a star shows a great struggle with circumstances.

On the Hepatica, internal illness, sometimes an operation.

CROSSES.

Crosses must be independent of the lines, not formed partly by them. An ill-made, uneven cross is a bad sign, but if well formed and clear it is not unfavourable.

A cross on the Mount of Jupiter, large and clear, signifies a happy marriage, or other gratified ambition. A small cross on the same Mount indicates the marriage ceremony.

A cross on Saturn's Mount reveals misfortune, generally connected with health. .

On the Mount of Apollo a cross points out a particular disappointment in connection with art or money.

On the Mount of Mercury, it shows a tendency to steal, or to take advantage of people.

On the Mount of Mars (under Mercury), great personal danger—it may be through accident, or enmity, but the injury will be caused by some individual.

On Mars (under Jupiter), the same mark shows a tendency to suicide.

On the Mount of Venus it denotes an unhappy love affair. If the cross appear on a line on this Mount, the loss of the person represented by the line is indicated.

A cross on Luna signifies danger at sea, or on water.

On the Quadrangle, an interest in, or aptitude for occultism and mystical subjects. This is called the " Mystic Cross."

A cross on the Triangle, an important event, necessitating a change.

A cross on the Life-line indicates a serious illness or accident.

On the Head-line, an injury to the head, by accident or otherwise, but is not so harmful as a star on this line.

On the Heart-line a cross denotes trouble through the affections.

On the Fate-line, it is the sign of an accidental change of circumstances causing trouble. If near, but not on the line, it will happen to a relative or friend with whom the " subject's " life is bound up.

A cross on the Hepatica indicates illness.

On the Line of Apollo, if clear and well made, shows unexpected acquisition of money—a " windfall."

ISLANDS.

An Island is made by a line dividing into two even lines and then re-uniting, but must be distinguished from cross lines. It is always a bad sign, wherever it may be found.

Transverse Islands are adverse influences.

An Island on the Life-line indicates severe illness. If in the left hand, hereditary. If in the right hand, it is caused by outward circumstances.

On the Head-line an island signifies delirium, or over-strained brain.

On the Heart-line, if the line shows no sign of physical weakness, the island will indicate an unfortunate attachment. The island may, however, point to organic disease, other signs being present.

An island on the Fate-line denotes an unhappy, and often an immoral attachment, when an "Influence-line" runs into it. If no such indication be near, the island will refer to health.

On the Apollo-line, loss of money, or bankruptcy. In the left hand, family loss. In the right hand, personal.

An island on the Hepatica is the indication of internal illness, and sometimes means cancer.

On any of the "Influence-lines" an island signifies sorrow through or illness of that person.

TRIANGLES.

Triangles are favourable signs, and show an aptitude for scientific pursuits.

On the Mount of Jupiter a triangle is an indication of success in a parliamentary or diplomatic career.

On Saturn, it shows an aptitude for occult science.

On Apollo, success in the medical profession—in scientific art.

On Mercury, success in any scientific calling or learned profession.

On the Mount of Mars a triangle denotes good generalship. Military honours.

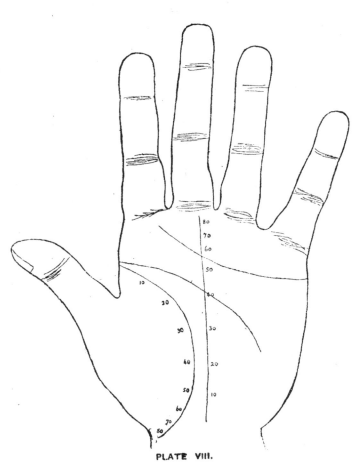

PLATE VIII.

MEASUREMENT OF TIME AND CALCULATION OF AGE.

On the Mount of Luna, intuition highly developed.

On the Mount of Venus, worldly prudence and calculation in regard to matrimony.

SQUARES.

Squares are usually marks of **preservation from accident, illness, or other danger.** But when found on the Mount of Venus they may indicate imprisonment. If perfectly formed, there will be a narrow escape of such, but if the square is broken incarceration is. probable. The square is a most important sign, as, when found near a star, broken line, or other warning, it signifies that the " subject " will escape the danger, or, at least, if hurt, will recover.

CIRCLES.

Circles are not often seen on the hands. **On the lines** they signify **misfortune,** but **on the Mounts** they are good, and denote **success** or **honour.**

On the Line of Heart a circle is a sign of blindness.

DOTS.

Dots, or spots, anywhere on the hand are **unfavourable.**

On the Head-line, and of a blue or black shade, they indicate typhus or typhoid fever.

Red dots on the Mounts signify wounds.

White dots on the Head-line, deafness.

On the Heart-line, weakness of that organ.

GRILLES.

Grilles represent **obstacles,** and frustrate the efforts towards success in the desire or aim signified by the Mount on which they are found.

If on Jupiter, they are a bar to social success and matrimonial happiness.

On Saturn, they bring misfortune.

On Apollo, they mean a striving after unattainable fame.

On the Mount of Mercury, dishonesty.

On Mars, a violent or sudden death.

On Luna, they cause much discontent, sadness, and anxiety.

On Venus, they signify danger of imprisonment, captivity, or restraint of personal freedom—such as would occur in a convent or asylum.

CHAINS.

Chains on any of the lines show weakness. They are usually found at the commencement of the line, and indicate :—

On the Life-line, delicacy in childhood.

On the Head-line, bronchial and throat troubles.

On the Heart-line, weakness of the organ.

A chain frequently encircles the second joint of the thumb, and in this position it signifies an argumentative disposition.

MEASUREMENT OF TIME.

Time and Age are calculated by drawing an imaginary line across the middle of the palm, and on the Fate-line, reckoning that point as 30. The age of 10 will be nearly on a level with the base of Luna, and the distance between that and 30, and above, can be marked off in spaces of five or ten years, up to the Saturn finger. But after 50 the spaces must be decreased.

On the Life-line the age is reckoned downwards—beginning under the Mount of Jupiter (see Plate VIII., p. 53). It is a help to the dating of any event, past or future, if the client will first disclose his present age, although this can often be discovered without the information.

CHAPTER VIII

How to Read the Hands

WHEN about to delineate the hands, the Palmist should take care not to touch them in the first instance, as much may be gathered from the natural inclination of the fingers.

The back of the hands should be considered first in order to ascertain the type to which they belong.

The nails next are to be particularly noted. By them, temper and the tendencies to some maladies are judged.

The length of the fingers, from the lowest knuckle (or joint) to the tip, must be measured and compared with the palm, from fingers to wrist, when the hand is turned over ; if viewed only from the front the fingers appear shorter than they really are.

The palms being now uppermost the natural position of the fingers will be observed. One or more may stand out prominently, fall behind the others, or curl up towards the palm. All such signs have meanings attached to them.

The hands may now be touched to judge of their consistency, whether firm or soft, but care must be taken to distinguish between a soft silky skin and general flabbiness of the hand. The former frequently accompanies a firm palm, and will not then denote indolence, but susceptibility to atmospheric changes, and other influences which affect the health.

When the fingers fall naturally wide apart it is a sign of unconventionality, a dislike to restraint of any kind. When close together, the " subject " is

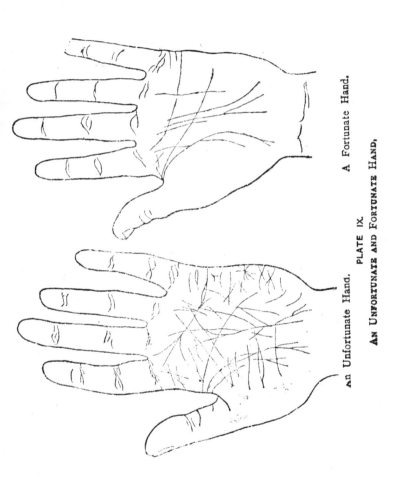

An Unfortunate Hand.   A Fortunate Hand.

PLATE IX.

AN UNFORTUNATE AND FORTUNATE HAND.

conventional and reserved in disposition. He will have no originality and will form his opinions on those of others.

A wide opening between the first and second fingers denotes originality and independence of thought. A wide space between the second and third fingers shows independence of circumstances, a " happy-go-lucky " nature. When tha third and fourth fingers are widely separated, independence of action is shown. In the left hand and not in the right " the subject " is naturally of a self-reliant nature, but has not been allowed to exercise it. In the right hand only, independence and self-confidence have been acquired.

Fingers curling towards the palm are indicative of great tenacity of purpose. These people do not lightly give up any enterprise or undertaking. They are given to collecting and hoarding, although not miserly. Avarice is only to be read when the thumb turns in towards the palm, when the fingers assume a claw-like outline, when the palm is narrow and flat, and the Heart-line and Mount of Venus poor. Fingers turning back from the palm show that the person is not to be depended upon. He will take things up energetically and enthusiastically at first, but will soon tire of an occupation, and cannot be trusted to carry out any scheme. He means well, but has no tenacity or stability.

There is something also to be learnt from the setting of the fingers. If all are on a level at the base, it promises well for the success of the individual, and indicates favourable circumstances for the development of inherent powers and qualities. Fingers straight and well developed, show evenness of mental balance. When crooked there is some want or twist in the character.

The inclination of the fingers towards each other is significant also, and the attributes of one will influence or neutralise the other. For example, Jupiter inclining to Saturn, will lose ambition, love of prominence, and will be under the power of destiny. Saturn leaning towards Apollo, will throw sadness into the artist's picture, or dull his colours; will cause the author to take up serious subjects, and will make of the actor a tragedian. Apollo leaning towards Mercury will turn artistic talents to practical account, thus in engineering or architecture, drawing will be used for business purposes. When one finger is relatively longer or more prominent than the others, if it rise towards the palm, or stand out from the hand in a marked manner, it is a great index of the general character, which will be moulded on the qualities the finger possesses. With a prominent Jupiter finger the person will always endeavour to come to the front, to rule and lead. He likes to stand well in the eyes of his fellow creatures. Saturn prominent will make him extremely careful, cautious and pessimistic. With Apollo to the front he will be ambitious of success in art, literature, or in acquiring wealth, if coupled with a short straight Head-line. Mercury dominant shows the capacity for using the talents. He will succeed best in business, science or diplomacy; or, if the Mercury finger is square, preceptive qualities are indicated, and the owner will do well as a teacher, professor, lecturer.

A dominant thumb gives great power over people and circumstances. Possessors of this are usually good organisers or commanders.

When the fingers of Apollo and Saturn are of equal length, speculative tendencies are revealed.

The fingers by themselves come next under

examination, each phalange being noted. By these the **talents and proclivities** can be ascertained; after which the Mounts must be observed, and felt, in order to determine which qualities are cultivated and which have been neglected. If firm to the touch, it shows development of that particular Mount, but if soft, its property has not been much used or encouraged. Thus much of the character will be unveiled, and a fair judgment can be **formed of the life** and, to a certain extent the **future career,** of the "subject," presuming that he follows the instincts and inclinations of his nature.

The lines are next closely inspected, the principal ones first. By these the past and present state of health is shown, the hereditary tendencies, the intellectual capacity, and the capability of affection. Also the events of life, past and future. Lastly, the minor lines and various signs are traced; these will give details and causes, and also indicate the dangers and influences to be avoided.

DIFFERENCE BETWEEN RIGHT AND LEFT HANDS.

Both hands must be viewed with care and compared, but **the right hand is the most important,** as, on it we read the facts of life, why the "subject" has succeeded, or why he has failed. From it we also see what use he has made of his talents and opportunities. We see the favourable growth of character, or retrogression, the development of hereditary tendencies, or the arrest of these, improvement in health or the reverse. By the right hand also we can in a measure judge what the future is likely to bring forth.

No palmist can, however, **with certainty predict**

the occurrences of life. We can only foresee the probable development of certain signs, and from the character, position, health, and other factors, draw deductions and give a forecast of what may follow.

The accurate statements so often made by palmists, regarding the future, are more frequently the result of clairvoyance, or intuitive power, which many people possess in a high degree, sometimes unknown to themselves, and which they unconsciously use. This is a gift which may be developed but cannot be acquired. Used in conjunction with a knowledge of palmistry it is exceedingly valuable.

The left hand is the hand of possibilities, of thought, and of heredity. On this we see the transmission of character and qualities from parents to their offspring.

Illnesses, diseases, and other tendencies marked on this hand may not develop in the " subject," but if the signs are there the possibility must be guarded against. If confirmed in the right hand, the danger is greater or the malady has already shown itself.

Characteristics and talents seen in the left hand are inherent, or latent in the individual, and we look at the right hand to see how far they have been cultivated or developed.

Characteristics, tastes, etc., marked in the right hand only, have been acquired and are foreign to the person's nature. Circumstances may have moulded his disposition as in the struggle of life a combative spirit is grafted upon a peaceable temper, or, the beautiful and artistic surroundings of a luxurious home, and cultured society, may refine, and create in a coarse nature, an appreciation of art and ideals transcending the natural sordidness of his early life.

The left hand is the hand of thought in this way, that the signs of marriage, disaster, fame, position, wealth and other indications seen thereon, and unconfirmed in the right are not facts, but disclose only the desires, ambitions, fears and worries that agitate the "subject's" mind. They may, in some cases, be read as relating not to the individual, but to a near relative or close friend.

When these signs are marked clearly in both hands, it is safe to state experiences already gone through, or events likely to occur, this according to the position of the sign and age of the person (see Plate VIII., p. 53). For instance, a star on the Mount of Luna in the left hand would indicate anxiety for some one travelling by sea, or the death by drowning, of a relative or dear friend.

If in both hands the disaster may happen to the individual himself, or he may narrowly escape such a calamity, in which case a "square" should appear close to the mark.

So it is with all other signs on the left hand, they are either from nervous apprehension, or from sympathy for the sufferer. Qualities and talents well defined in the left hand and less marked in the right, indicate the want of cultivation of these gifts.

Illnesses and diseases marked on the right hand only are not inherited, but have been brought on by the mode of life, by accident, rashness or neglect of health.

In closing this chapter, however, I would warn the student never to judge by one sign alone. The whole hand must be read, opposing influences or mitigating signs taken into account, and allowance made for temperament, health, and other factors before judgment is pronounced.

PART II.

Showing how the Science may be used in ordinary life.

CHAPTER I

Hints to Parents and Guardians

HAVING placed before my readers in the foregoing chapters sufficient knowledge of the subject to enable them to understand the terms and nomenclature employed in Palmistry, I shall now proceed to point out the application of the study to everyday life. It is not until about the age of fourteen, that the hand of either sex exhibits clearly, in external appearance, the distinctive qualities which will mould the character and influence the future life, but before the age of seven, assistance in the method of training the child may be obtained by a careful inspection of the tendencies displayed by the hand.

The hand and mind of the little one being then of so plastic a nature, it is easier to check, or encourage qualities that may have an effect upon the after life, than at a later date when the characteristics are stronger, and confirm the adage that " the child is father of the man." The power of altering the form of the hand, through moral training, may be doubted, but I maintain that it is possible to a certain extent.

When a man has reason to be proud of himself, his position or attainments, he straightens his figure, holds his head up, and walks with steady step. On the other hand, when conscious of inferiority, or when down-trodden by the circumstances of life, his head falls, and his figure droops in sympathy with the attitude of his mind.

So it is with the hand. **We cannot alter** the anatomical structure, but **we can correct** the natural pose of the fingers, and other signs, which to a Palmist mean so much.

Through any sustained effort of will-power, the thumb will stand out from the rest of the hand. The opportunity for self-assertion, or command, being attained, the finger of Jupiter will, unconsciously to the owner, become a prominent feature.

The exercise of moral and physical courage, and any occupation which strengthens the nerves, will harden the Mount of Mars, and cause all superfluous lines to disappear. The cultivation of the various qualities will uniformly develop the respective mounts, whereas the degradation of the same qualities will have the effect of effacing, or over-developing these, and the hand will assume a different appearance.

When a child's hand is much lined, with Head and Life-lines (see Plate III., p. 27) joined for some distance, the palm hollow, and the fingers long and pointed, the little one will be of a highly nervous, sensitive, timid nature and will require encouragement and care, otherwise he will shrink into himself, suffer alone—for he fears ridicule—and the

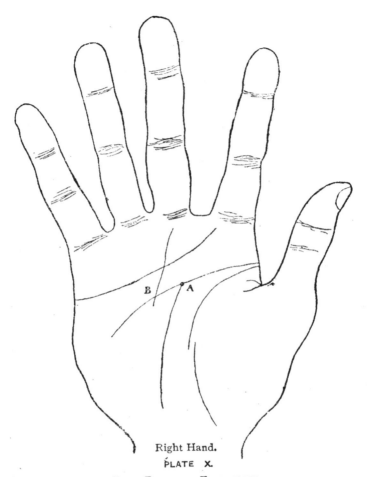

Right Hand.

PLATE X.

FROM PERSONAL EXPERIENCE.

A. Blue dot on Head-line shows severe attack of **Typhus Fever.**
Fate line stops on Head-line at that point ; career was **checked**
by the illness.

B. Fate-line shows fresh start in life. Subject left **America and**
came to England.

(Seen in the hand of a Professional Singer.)

weaknesses of character will increase instead of lessen. A little flattery, or spoken appreciation, will not spoil this nature, it is what the child wants, and will accept with gratitude, and not as his due.

If the Head and Life-lines be divided in the right hand, he will probably outgrow his early timidity and want of self-confidence.

A child who has Head and Life-lines wide apart in both hands, a firm, flat, unlined palm, the fingers well spread out and the tips either spatulate or square, will, on the contrary, be all the better for a little suppression and restraint, particularly if the fingers be short and the thumb heavy, which would, with the other signs, indicate rash impulses, a contempt for danger and disregard of authority.

When, in a child's hand, the Head-line is broken, it is an indication that the brain is not over-strong, even though the child exhibit great intelligence or precocity, perhaps more especially so in this case, as mental activity is frequently found in conjunction with physical weakness. Care should be taken that he is not over-worked, and plenty of time for bodily recreation, or rest, should be afforded him.

When a child displays great irritability of temper, the hand may be scanned for the purpose of discovering whether it proceeds from weakness of nerves, from any special complaint, or purely from inherited bad temper. If the latter, the child must be taught to suppress and control it, if from the former causes the physical remedy must be found and applied.

The habit of untruthfulness is one that is acquired at an early age, and it is difficult sometimes to discriminate whether it is wilful misstatement on the part of the child, or whether it is merely the effect of too vivid an imagination. Children in their games are so much accustomed to "make-believe," and the little brains are constantly receiving impressions and information they cannot reason out for themselves, that they call upon the power of fancy to fill up the gaps made through their limited experience, and can always find a solution for their own little problems which suffices for themselves. This creative faculty induces the practice of embellishing and exaggerating. Care therefore should be observed in the treatment of children with a highly developed Mount of Luna (see Plate II., p. 21) and a long sloping Head-line (see Plate III., p. 27) the signs of great mental activity and imagination.

A child possessing a soft palm and pointed fingers is naturally of an indolent, dreamy disposition; its habits of inattention and indifference will be trying to parent and teacher, but judicious training will do much to eradicate the tendencies of this nature.

The particular gifts, virtues, and evil propensities of the child may easily be discovered through a knowledge of Palmistry, and the proper direction of the life and development of character be given at an early age, instead of waiting until the faults become confirmed, when the task will be harder for parent and child alike.

CHAPTER II

On Training Youth and Choosing a Profession

MUCH valuable time is lost through parents not knowing, or not trying to find out, what their boys and girls are best fitted for, and so starting them in unsuitable careers.

A boy is often forced into a profession or business distasteful to him, simply because there happens to be an opening in his father's office—or the parents have a liking for some particular profession—an ambition to see their son occupy a certain post, regardless of his fitness, or his personal desires.

Lives are sometimes spoilt, through an error of judgment on the part of the parents, which might otherwise have been usefully and pleasantly spent.

It is easy enough to choose a profession for them when children at an early age show some aptitude for invention, engineering, or research, a talent for music, painting, or other art; but if the boy or girl has not developed any special gift, or expressed a preference for any path in life, the hand will point to the direction in which the natural bent will find scope for development, and the training should be in accordance with intellectual capacity, temperament, health, strength and tastes; thus we should have better work done, and more contented workers.

When we find the hand broad, firm, unlined, the fingers wide apart—the tips being spatulate or square—it is useless and even cruel to put that boy to desk or humdrum routine work. He loves open-air life, movement, variety, and will not work steadily in an office, or if he does, it is after severe training, and the suppression of natural inclinations. A boy with a hand of this description should be a soldier, a sailor, an engineer, an agriculturist, or follow some calling in which activity of body may be combined with brain work.

Those most suited for indoor occupations have narrow hands, long, pointed or conic fingers rather close together. The daily round and monotony will not irritate them in the same way, and they rather like to have their work cut out for them, not having so much originality and love of freedom as those with outspread hands, but they are more patient and painstaking.

A hand in which the chief points are—a strong thumb, straight Head-line (see Plate III., p. 27), flat palm, straight spatulate Mercury finger, and large nails, will show capability for business, and if combined with these, the fingers are on a level and the Apollo and Fate-lines (see Plate III., p. 27) good, the boy is likely to be successful.

A hand with a prominent Jupiter finger and mount will like to take the lead, and will endeavour to do so in whatever position the owner may be placed; but the professions most suited for him are those in which he can supervise others, he is essentially gregarious, and would be miserable if isolated. The church, the diplomatic service, any occupation pertaining to the scholastic, the law, or public office, would meet the requirements of a Jupiterian.

When Saturn rules, there is less desire for prominence. This boy will not object to a solitary, monotonous life, he rather likes to get away, for a time, from the "madding crowd." He may have a talent for invention or mathematics, and the occupations he is best suited for are :—agriculture and anything connected with the management of land or property, surveying, prospecting, exploring, colonising, he is well adapted for, and might also start tea or coffee plantations.

When Apollo is dominant in the hand it indicates **a taste for art or literature.** Boys having this finger and mount well developed, will most readily become doctors, dentists, chemists, artists or actors, or they may take up literature as a means of livelihood, if the head-line is long and deep.

The Mars type make **good soldiers, sailors, sportsmen,** and are fitted for occupations connected with a military or sea-faring life—for employment where horses are required, and they also become veterinary surgeons from choice. Among the lower classes they choose the occupations of coachman, groom, jockey, circus-rider, cabman, bus-driver, and so on. They have constructive power also and might take up engineering.

Governed by Mercury, a boy will have the attributes that fit him for **almost any path of life.** The capacity for using the talents belongs to this finger. A person may possess talents, but unless he has a certain amount of Mercury in his composition, he will not be able to use them to much advantage. Without Mercury, he will be dilatory, letting his chances go, or will fail to see where his opportunities lie. He has no enterprise, and will only succeed by some lucky chance or if taken in hand by some stronger nature and placed where little effort on his part is required.

As a class, Mercurians are hopeful and not afraid to venture, even when disappointment comes they are not discouraged, but will try again and again. The fancy of a Mercurian may incline him to **science,** and if so he will devote himself to research, and probably make a name for himself, or at least he will do good work. Business enterprise and capabilities are particularly to be found in people of **Mercurial temperament.** They do well on the Stock Exchange, and as teachers, clerks, accountants they are bound to succeed, having special aptitude for these callings.

When the dominant characteristics are those of Luna it will be difficult to find a suitable profession or occupation for this boy. He will be imaginative, unpractical, discontented and capricious, and will probably show no particular talent unless it be for writing. In such a case it should be cultivated. The Mount of Luna giving great imagination, his talent will probably make of him a novelist, dramatist or poet. He may also display a taste for collecting curios which might be turned to account in some post connected with the arrangement of a museum or anything of a similar nature.

Venus being the prominent mount in a hand, the "subject" will probably show some talent for music, vocal or instrumental according to the development of the lower angles of the thumb (see Plate IV., Frontispiece). He will be fond of travelling and of pleasure—his inclinations will be towards painting, music, singing and elocution. The trades that would suit him are those of florist, watchmaker, jeweller, musical instrument maker, and so forth.

The foregoing remarks on the different types and forms of hands, apply also to girls in a modified measure.

CHAPTER III

On the Professions and other Occupations

D'ARPENTIGNY, a French military officer, who first tabulated the system of chirognomy, claims to have come upon his discovery by Divine Inspiration. His biographer tells us how his attention was first drawn to the subject when on a visit to Spain, through having his own hands read by a Moorish gipsy. In later years he became acquainted with a rich land owner, who, being greatly interested in the exact sciences, gathered round him mathematicians, mechanicians, geometricians, and those who studied kindred subjects. His wife, however, favoured art, and delighted to invite artists, and people of artistic taste, to her house.

D'Arpentigny was a frequent guest at the parties of both husband and wife, and having beautiful hands himself, was struck with the diversity of form in those of the other visitors. He observed a marked contrast between the artists and mechanicians, the fingers of artists being smooth, while those of the scientists were invariably knotted. Upon this foundation he began to work, and evolved a theory which subsequent experiment and observation strengthened, until he gradually accumulated sufficient material to form a basis for the science, which has been carried on by Desbarrolles and others.

From their studies we are able to assign to the different professions and callings of life the type of hand containing the necessary characteristics and qualities for successful practice; or the adaptability for certain occupations.

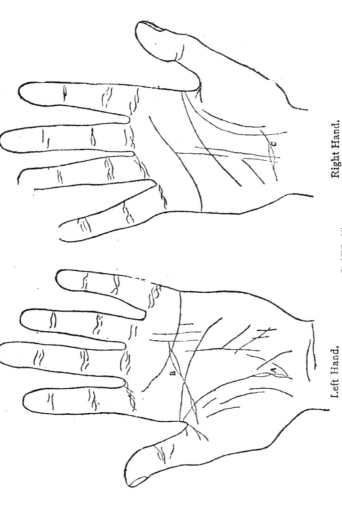

Left Hand.   Right Hand.

PLATE XI.

FROM PERSONAL EXPERIENCE.

A. Double islands on Life-line near the Fate-line in left hand show the death of both parents at an early age.
B. Serious trouble caused by a member of the family, entailing monetary loss.
C. Transverse island in right hand indicates an adverse influence during childhood (an aunt in this case).

There are, however, many "all-round" clever people who combine in their persons the talents and capabilities that fit them for almost any career, and who sometimes possess apparently opposing instincts and elements. General Baden Powell, the hero of Mafeking, is an example of this. He might with equal success have taken up the peaceful professions of actor, artist, or author, instead of turning his talents to the art of warfare. Earl Roberts can wield the pen as well as the sword; and numerous other instances might be found.

Music and art are constantly seen in combination, and the art of healing frequently accompanies a talent for drawing, painting, or acting. In the case of people thus gifted it will be difficult to decide which profession they are likely to be most successful in, or which they have taken up. All we can do is to show by the system of chirology the qualities that go to form the typical character in the various employments.

THE MEDICAL PROFESSION.

An ordinary practitioner has usually the spatulate type of hand (showing action), fingers wide apart (unconventionality). He should have a high amount of Mercury for quick diagnosis, and science lines on this Mount (see Plate IV., Frontispiece). A strong thumb (determination), good Head-line, sloping, but not too much (intellectual capacity).

As, in general practice, the manner and personal influence of a medical man have almost as much to do with his success as the ability he possesses, a doctor will do well who has a pointed finger of Mercury (tact). Also good Mounts of Venus and Luna, which will give him benevolence and sympathy. If in addition he has the line of

Intuition (see Plate III., p. 27), it will greatly aid him. By telepathy, or the transmission of thought from one mind to another, now an accepted fact, he will be able to read his patient's mind, to enter into his feelings, and in some cases through the same power, discover the seat of disease.

A SURGEON'S HAND.

For this the required characteristics are :— Long fingers (giving detail). Spatulate type (action). Second knot developed on all the fingers (order and method). Firm palm (energy, force, courage). Head-line clear and deep (concentration and a practical mind). And the "Science lines" on Mercury.

A PHYSICIAN AND SPECIALIST.

Long fingers (detail). Conic type (thought). First knot of all the fingers developed (order and method in ideas). Good Head-line (intellect). Luna well placed (imagination properly directed). Good Mount of Venus (benevolence). The Science lines on Mercury (aptitude for the profession).

A HOSPITAL NURSE

should have the following :—Spatulate type of hand (activity). Firm palm (energy and courage). Science lines on Mercury (aptitude for the profession). Good Mounts of Venus and Luna (sympathy and benevolence).

THE LAW.

The leading characteristics of a general practitioner are :—Fingers long and close (detail, and the observance of form and rule—red-tapism). Long straight thumb (will-power and logic). Straight Head-line (practical common sense), Forked Head-line (dissimulation — the power to conceal, or disguise the truth in order to support a weak case). Flat palm (combativeness).

A BARRISTER.

The same points which distinguish the lawyer mark the barrister, but with the difference that the fingers of Jupiter and Saturn are wide apart; also those of Apollo and Mercury (independence of thought and action). A spatulate Apollo finger and turned back thumb, will give him dramatic talent, and a long first phalange of Mercury will add eloquence to his pleading.

A JUDGE

should have long conic fingers (detail and thought). A wide quadrangle (the space between Head and Heart-lines), this will make him broad-minded and enable him to see both sides of a question. Good Head-line (intellect). Long first phalange of Mercury (power of words). Straight Jupiter finger and good Mount of Apollo (justice tempered with mercy).

THE CLERGY.

The leading features in the hand of a High Church clergyman are :—Long fingers, rather close together, for he is conventional. A dominant and conic finger of Jupiter which give religious sentiments and feelings. A good Apollo finger (artistic taste in religious ceremonies). First phalange of Mercury long (power of words— eloquence). Luna developed (imagination). The Mount of Venus good, and the angles of music present (see Plate IV., Frontispiece); these will give him a liking for musical services. He has usually a poor thumb and a pointed Mercury finger, as he does not rule so much by strength of will as by persuasion. With a long Heart-line rising between Jupiter and Saturn, he will sacrifice himself for duty or religion.

LOW CHURCH CLERGYMEN AND DISSENTERS.

These have heavy turned-out thumbs, they like to govern by strength of will and personality, and are more dogmatic than their High Church brethren. The finger of Apollo is poor, they do not care for display. The finger of Jupiter is good, giving earnestness in religion. The type is either square or spatulate with broad thick palm and fingers wide apart. They are unconventional, and like freedom and space, even open-air services when practicable.

A THEOLOGIAN.

The knot of philosophy will be present, showing investigation, order in ideas. A dominant finger of Jupiter, turning research towards religious matters. Luna developed and fingers pointed (thoughtful imagination). Long Head-line, sloping a little (intellectual capacity).

THE ARTISTIC HAND.

A good straight and long finger of Apollo (art) is the first requisite. Long first phalange of Apollo (for form). Wide first phalange of Apollo (for colour). A pointed finger of Jupiter (inspiration). Good Mount of Luna (imagination). A space between Jupiter and Saturn fingers (originality).

THE SCULPTOR'S HAND.

Fingers inclining to square (realism). Rather large hand (detail). Good Apollo finger (art). With spatulate tip and long first phalange (form).

AN ANIMAL PAINTER

has spatulate fingers (life and movement). Long, straight finger of Apollo (art). The Apollo Mount developed and encroaching on Mercury (love of animals).

AN IMPRESSIONIST.

Pointed and smooth fingers (impression, inspiration, idealism). Small hand (no detail). Good Apollo finger (art). Mount of Mercury developed (imitation).

A MINIATURE PAINTER

has a large hand and long fingers (capacity for detail). Good finger of Apollo with first phalange developed (art).

THE HISTORICAL PAINTER.

Long fingers (giving detail). Straight Head-line (practical ideas). Rather square Apollo finger (truth in depicting scenes).

THE PAINTER OF IDEAL SCENES

has a high Mount of Luna encroaching on the Bracelet (see Plate IV., Frontispiece). A long sloping Head-line, both of which will give fanciful ideas. Pointed fingers without knots (thought and inspiration). Good Apollo finger (art) with spatulate tip and long first phalange (form).

Painters with a square Apollo finger depict realistic scenes. With a crooked finger of Saturn leaning towards Apollo, morbid pictures with unpleasant details. With high Mounts of Mars, they will paint battle scenes, animal combats and so forth.

AN ARCHITECT.

An architect should have a long straight spatulate finger of Apollo (art). The first phalange particularly long (for form and design). A straight Head-line (practicability) and a long finger of Saturn (calculation).

MUSIC.

A high Mount of Venus implies a love of Melody. The power to use the talent of Music is shown in the Angles on the outside of the thumb (see Plate IV., Frontispiece). The higher angle denotes a correct ear for time. The lower represents vocal powers. For execution supple fingers are required in addition to above.

A VIOLINIST

has the "artist's hand," large and supple, with music developed.

A PIANIST OR ORGANIST

spatulate or square fingers, broad palm, very supple small hand and music developed. (Note— a large hand will choose a small instrument, a small hand a large one. Also in painting, a small hand will select a large canvas and ambitious subjects; a large hand on the contrary will paint in miniature and detail).

A SINGER

has the signs of music, with the lower angle of the thumb well marked, and above it the Mount of Venus firm, if the voice is used.

A COMPOSER OF MUSIC.

For composition square fingers are desirable. A straight Head-line in addition to the musical characteristics.

THE STAGE.

An actor's hand requires a good spatulate finger of Apollo (action in art). The other fingers are generally spatulate, but not necessarily so. Fingers wide apart and flexible (adaptability). The thumb turned back at the tip. High Mounts of Luna and Mercury (imagination and imitation).

COMEDY

is seen in an actor's hand when the Mount of Mercury is very high, and the nail on the Mercury finger small.

TRAGEDY

is shown in a prominent finger of Saturn, and the Mount of Saturn displaced, inclining to Apollo, and combined with acting characteristics.

When the Head-line in an actor's hand turns up towards Mercury it usually means success.

THE DIPLOMATIC SERVICE.

The salient points in the hand of a diplomatist are, a high Mount of Jupiter (gregariousness, ambition, self-assertion). A good Head-line, but slightly forked (dissimulation). A long pointed finger of Mercury (tact, persuasive powers). Bright nails (quick grasp of the situation).

THE ARMY.

A soldier's hand has usually short fingers, spatulate or square, the Mounts of Mars firm (courage, endurance, promptitude), and Mercury developed (buoyancy, hope and cheerfulness), a heavy thumb, few lines, a hard skin and flat palm (combativeness). For command Jupiter must be long and prominent. With a prominent Saturn finger soldiers will follow, but will not lead, neither will they rise from the ranks. Lord Kitchener's hands are not typical of the fighting soldier. The fingers are long and conic, and in this they bear out the Palmist's theory of the index of forethought, organisation, and attention to detail, Lord Kitchener's special characteristics; the thumb is high set and well developed, showing reasoning faculties and determination. As in all great and successful men, the finger of Mercury is conspicuous. The hand indicates an artistic nature, and the lines betray a greater depth of feeling and impressionability than the world gives him credit for. He is not the mere " fighting machine " his enemies and critics have called him, but has also a soft side to his character.

THE NAVY.

A sailor has much the same characteristics as the soldier, but in addition the Mount of Luna must be high and firm, and the palm broad, which will give a love of the sea and open air life.

LITERATURE.

A literary hand should display a well developed conic finger of Jupiter (inspiration, receptive faculties). A long first phalange of Mercury (command of language). Good Head-line (intellectual powers). Good Mount of Luna (imagination).

A literary critic has short nails (criticism), a prominent Jupiter finger, and the Mount of Luna very slightly developed.

OCCUPATIONS AND TRADES.

AN ENGINEER.

The hands of an engineer require spatulate fingers (action, love of motion and machinery, practicability). They have usually broad palms and flat mounts.

A STOCKBROKER

should possess the "speculative" hand, that is, having the fingers of Saturn and Apollo nearly of the same height, spatulate type, straight Head-line (intellectual powers turned to business account).

A MATHEMATICIAN

has double knots on all the fingers, which are long usually. A thin palm. Long straight Head-line. Heavy Saturn finger with the second knot particularly developed (calculation).

AN AGRICULTURIST.

Hard stiff hand with broad palm (giving a preference for open air occupation). A long finger of Saturn, the second phalange of which should be distinctly long.

AN AGENT.

The characteristics of this hand are a long Saturn finger, showing a nature that will work under others. A straight, but not prominent Jupiter finger, which will indicate willingness to accept responsibility, but no desire to rule or lead.

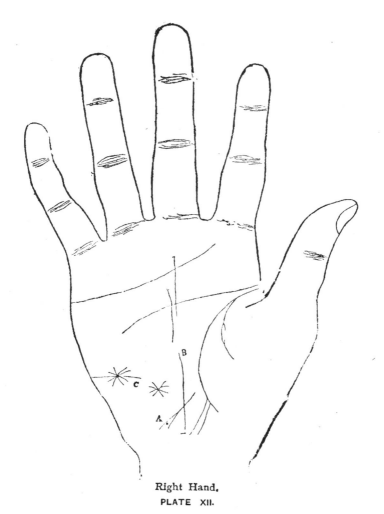

Right Hand.

PLATE XII.

FROM PERSONAL EXPERIENCE.

A.—A. Signs indicating death of fiancé.
B. Stopping of Fate-line at 25.
C. Stars on Luna, one being on voyage line the cause of the alteration in career.

Explanation.

On voyage from America "Subject" was shipwrecked, losing mother and sister and narrowly escaped drowning herself. For some years afterwards she lost the power of walking.

CHAPTER IV

On the Hands of the Working Classes

IN a minor degree the same traits of character, propensities, and proclivities show themselves in the hands of the manual toilers of the world, as in those of highly educated and cultured people. A particularly marked and developed quality indicates a man able to rise above his environment, and take a higher place in the social scale.

The taste for art, science, and other developments of civilization, although only elementary, is displayed as in the hands of the cultured classes, and will influence the individual choice of employment—that is, if freedom of will is permitted and the boy or girl is not forced into some uncongenial occupation.

Pointed or conic fingers are a sign of high breeding, in so far, that they show descent from ancestors who have been removed from the necessity for manual labour; delicacy of feeling and fastidiousness of taste having been cultivated through generations, amid surroundings of elegance and comfort; consequently this form of hand is mostly to be found in the upper classes, where refinement of features is so noticeable; but, as with the face also, delicately fashioned hands are occasionally met with in the lower ranks of life, indicating innate refinement, perhaps inherited from some progenitor of higher birth and breeding.

When, among the lower orders, we come across long pointed fingers, we may be sure these people will avoid, if possible, all rough and dirty work. The men will select occupations such as those of miller, carpenter or tailor; and the women will choose the light employments of flower maker, florist, milliner, and so forth.

Manual workers, such as **plumbers, butchers, labourers,** will be found with spatulate finger tips, **broad, hard unlined hands,** showing little sensitiveness of feeling, and it is fortunate for the rest of the community that there are such people in the world to do all this necessary work.

Among the upper or cultured classes, conversely, we find the spatulate type, but it is seldom purely so, the fingers will be varied, and other signs of refinement, culture, and education will present themselves —the hand will be more flexible, fingers and mounts more evenly developed, the lines more numerous, and other indications of " class " will be marked thereon. The spatulate type will then merely indicate the action and energy belonging to the temperament of the individual, ability to **overcome obstacles,** and fastidious distaste, in the pursuance of the science or work that is taken up ; for this reason **doctors and nurses should have spatulate fingers.**

The following are a few examples giving the indications of suitability for different occupations.

Hands with prominent Apollo and Mercury fingers will make good tailors, shoemakers, cabinet makers, dressmakers, milliners, and are suited for any trade in which a certain amount of artistic taste and design is required.

Hands with long fingers, and the Mounts of Venus, Apollo and Mercury developed, will do fine work. They are well adapted for watchmakers, jewellers, lacemakers, and other employments requiring delicate handling.

The hands of a gardener are usually spatulate, with long knotted fingers, large hard palm, long Head-line, the Mount of Luna developed, but no Mercury.

For landscape gardening a good Apollo finger is required as evidence of talent for artistic design.

CHAPTER V

On Maladies and Diseases

ONE of the most important uses to which Palmistry may be put is that of tracing symptoms of disease. The following signs, which have been well tested and verified, if not actually the evidence of present illness, are always a warning of the tendency to the special malady of which the mark is distinctive.

Good health is shown by a firm, smooth texture of the skin, cool but not moist, the principal lines pale and clear, and the absence of fine short lines and other marks. Although the "subject" may be in the enjoyment of good health, the special type to which he belongs will indicate the ailments and accidents he is most prone to. If this fact were noted and acted upon, much suffering might be avoided.

A hand covered with a number of small "hair" lines shows extreme sensitiveness and irritability of the nervous system. With very red lines and dry skin there is a tendency to fever. These people should be warned not to expose themselves to infection. Wide pale lines show weakness and anæmia. Yellow skin and lines indicate internal illnesses, a bilious constitution, tendency to jaundice. Lines irregularly coloured—fluctuating health. A soft, silky skin—rheumatic affections. The skin frayed round the nails shows delicacy, and small illnesses. Small lines on the first phalanges of the fingers denote the beginning of ill-health.

Small half-moons, or over-developed—also red nails are evidences of bad circulation.

Typhoid fever is indicated by a black or blue dot on the Head-line.

Gastric fever by a red dot on the Hepatica.

Scarlet fever by a small circle or square on the Life-line enclosing a cross.

Brain fever is shown by a broken or islanded Head-line.

Overworked brain by a frayed Head-line.

Rheumatic fever, soft skin, fine lines crossing the Heart-line under Saturn.

Epilepsy, one indication of this malady is pointed, crooked fingers and the mounts under the fingers shrunken.

Nervous headaches, numerous small lines crossing the Head-line, and dents on the Line.

Bilious headaches, small lines cutting through the Hepatica.

Gout, frayed Hepatica Line.

Consumption, high curved nails, the Heart-line " feathered " from Saturn to Jupiter.

Heart-disease (sudden seizure), black dots on the Heart-line. Heart-disease (consequent on rheumatic fever), large island on the Heart-line. Lingering heart-disease, pale, blurred Heart-line, " feathered " from Saturn to the Percussion, or the Heart-line chained, looped or broken.

Disordered Liver, damp, soft hand. Yellow lines, nails spotted, and rather red. Hepatica broken.

Bright's Disease, small white dents on the Head-line near the Mount of Mars.

Paralysis, a star on the Mount of Saturn lines, crossing the Heart-line, soft skin, hard, flat nails.

Spine Disease, an island on the Life-line under Saturn.

Tumour, cancer and similar diseases, islands on the Hepatica and the Head-line turning up.

Blindness from over straining of the sight, a dent or circle under Apollo. Blindness from accident, a star on the Heart-line under Apollo.

Dropsy, a star on the Mount of Luna.

Insanity, a cross on the Mount of Luna, a long sloping Head-line, Mount of Luna very low (or too high), Saturn Mount absent, and the finger of Saturn crooked, are the various signs of lunacy, or a tendency thereto—but great discrimination must be exercised in reading these.

Hysteria is shown by a soft palm, chains, and many fine lines—also by a distorted outline of the hand.

Bronchial Diseases and throat delicacy—by a chained Head-line under Jupiter—by the arching of the Head-line under the finger of Saturn.

Skin Diseases, or a tendency thereto—a soft skin and fluted nails.

Deafness is shown by dents on the Head-line.

Weakness of sight by dots on the Heart-line.

Indigestion, white spots on the nails.

General delicacy, very thin nails, and the hand covered with a net-work of fine lines.

DISEASES, ACCIDENTS, ETC., TO WHICH THE VARIOUS TYPES RENDER ONE LIABLE.

Jupiter rules the Head, Lungs and Throat. The illnesses Jupiterians are subject to are inflammation of the lungs, pleurisy, quinsy and all throat affections. Also gout and apoplexy—as they indulge in "high living." They are specially liable to accidents through horses.

Saturn governs the ears, teeth and spleen. Saturnians are liable to biliousness, rheumatism, skin diseases, paralysis, and deafness. They lose their teeth early after much suffering. They are prone to accidents through falls from buildings, to drowning and to suicide.

Apollo has an influence over eyes, limbs, spine and heart, and causes liability to diseases of the heart, spinal complaint, loss of sight, and injury to limbs.

Mercury governs the brain, liver and kidneys. Mercurians are liable to insanity, impediments of speech, and diseases of liver and kidneys.

Mars. People under the influence of Mars are liable to acute fevers, and diseases connected with internal organs; to burns, and accidents from fire and fire-arms.

Luna, the diseases belonging to this mount are dropsy, consumption, lunacy and others. It renders the " subject " liable to accidents by water.

Venus governs the generative organs—the diseases of this mount are more especially hysteria, and feminine disorders.

In cases of ill-health where symptoms are not clearly defined, and doctors are sometimes baffled in locating the malady, Palmistry might render assistance. Temperament and the mode of life have so much to do with the welfare of the body, and a correct idea of these cannot always be deduced from the manner and surroundings of the patient, but an inspection of the hand will disclose secrets sometimes.

A woman may apparently be living on the best of terms with her husband, and to outward appearance hers may be what is termed a happy marriage, but a study of her hand may reveal the cause of failing health—worry, anxiety of mind, disappointed affection. Although she may strive to conceal the skeleton in the cupboard, the lines will disclose reasons for jealousy and indignation on the part of a wife; or the daily friction of the nerves, through living with a partner of uncongenial nature.

If the hand is much lined, the Head-line long, Luna soft and low, and the fingers crooked, the patient is probably fanciful, hysterical, and dwells too much upon grievances and troubles, making mountains out of mole-hills.

A hand with a poor thumb and Mercury finger, and no Mount of Mercury, has very little recuperative power. It shows a want of will, spirit, and ability to throw off diseases and troubles. These people will be difficult to cure because they will not help themselves.

A deep line on the Mount of Mars (under Jupiter) from the base of the thumb to the Life-line shows an intense shrinking from physical pain, and with a much-lined hand, extreme sensitiveness to pain, either mental or bodily.

People of a sanguine temperament—which is evidenced by a prominent finger and Mount of Apollo, and a wide space between the Apollo and Saturn fingers — will make little of their ailments, and if they possess a good Mount of Mercury also, will recover quickly, hope, cheerfulness, and buoyancy being pronounced elements in their constitution.

When the Mounts of Mars are firm and well developed, and the thumb strong, the patient will show great courage and endurance, and can make up his mind to undergo suffering, or operations if needful. Hereditary taints and tendencies can be seen in the hand, which are perhaps unknown to the patient himself, and may aid the doctor in finding a solution of what seems otherwise mysterious. He will also be able to tell from the

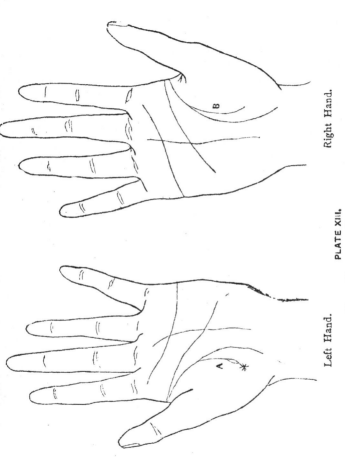

Left Hand.

Right Hand.

PLATE XIII.

FROM PERSONAL EXPERIENCE.

A. Venus influence-line with star and island. Seen in the left hand of a lady whose husband met with a railway accident and was nearly killed.

B. The same line in right hand being clear shows that he recovered.

hand whether the patient is suited for the work he is engaged upon, and might, perhaps, suggest a different occupation for him. Finally he will see from different indications on the hand the inclination to self-indulgence, intemperance, and so on, which he may have no opportunity of discovering by other means.

Other arguments might be found, but these few will serve to support the statement that Palmistry would be a valuable aid to the Medical Profession.

CHAPTER VI

On Marriage

IT is a difficult, and perhaps superfluous undertaking to give advice on the all-important subject of marriage, as the majority of people follow their own inclinations regardless of consequences. They are guided by the feelings of the moment, and often rashly enter the Holy Bonds of Matrimony, taking the step against their better judgment. George Eliot has said "that men and women are like hemispheres, that unhappy marriages are the result of the wrong halves coming together." And it is only when the proper "hemispheres" meet that the orb is complete, and marriage is, what Heaven meant it to be—the union of Soul— a bond not made for this world alone. When dispositions do not fit each other friction is caused; the constant irritation spoils the temper, and wears away self-control and patience, and open disagreement is a frequent consequence. These same people having other partners might be happy enough, but alas! such mistakes are only discovered when too late.

The science of Palmistry might, with advantage, be here called into requisition. It aids us in the criticism and analysis of self. It points out the temperament and tendencies we have inherited, the faults to be cured, and the moral dangers to be avoided. If we follow its guidance it will show us the qualities we lack, and enable us to discover whether, in the character of the chosen partner there are the counteracting influences, the sympathies and powers that we require for the favourable development of our own nature, and the cultivation of the best that is in us. Palmistry will also disclose the faults and failings in the character of those with whom we purpose casting in our lot, and, whether it be in matrimony or any other alliance, we can gauge by the strength or weakness, and by the opposing forces the hand displays, the amount of happiness, or success, that is likely to ensue from partnership.

MEN'S HANDS AND MARRIAGE.

A few hints on the indications of characteristics to be avoided may be serviceable to the woman who thinks seriously of marriage, but it must be remembered that **one sign alone is not sufficient** from which to form a correct judgment. Every point must be considered and weighed, otherwise we may do an injustice. A **hot temper,** for instance, may be clearly manifested by the shape and colour of the nails, but if the Mount of Mars is firm, and the thumb strong, **self-control** and strength of will are there, and anger will be kept **within proper bounds.**

Before entering into an engagement it is wise to ascertain the ambitions, aspirations, and **tastes or the suitor.** These are inscribed upon his hand, and a girl can, if versed in Palmistry, form some idea of the company the man frequents, the pursuits he is likely to take up, whether his disposition is adapted to hers or not ; and should she find his moral character weak, she must ask herself if she has sufficient strength of will and affection to influence and restrain his more pliable nature. From the man's hand she can find out **his chances of success** or the cause of failure, whether it proceeds from inability,

want of perseverance, weakness of health or nerves, or other opposing circumstances. She will then know what allowances to make, what encouragement or stimulus to give, and she will be able to judge of her own future prospects, to curtail her ambitions if necessary, or to fit herself for duties she may require to undertake, and so become a **real help-mate** to the man she has chosen.

When, in a man's hand, the finger of Jupiter is short and crooked, the first phalange of the thumb heavy, and the second phalange poor, the lower mounts over-developed, the heart-line short and without branches—it would be well not to marry that person. He is passionate, tyrannical, has no sense of honour or duty, and **selfishness** is the ruling power of his life.

If the line of **Intemperance** is deeply marked in both hands, the thumb is short and weak, and the Mount of Mars (under Jupiter) soft, the woman who accepts this man may find she has married a drunkard; the tendency will be an inherited taint, and there is little hope of reform, as the poor thumb shows weakness of will, and the soft Mars a lack of self-government, the inability to fight against any form of degeneration.

A man with short, square, white nails, the Mounts of Mars high, and the thumb thick and clubbed, **will not make a kind husband.** These signs indicate an ungovernable temper, a propensity for picking quarrels, and a revengeful nature.

Unless a girl is prepared meekly to submit to her "lord and master," let her **avoid** a man with a long, broad first phalange of the thumb, and heavy development of the joint, the second phalange being insignificant, the finger of Jupiter long and prominent, Luna and Venus low. Such a man likes to lead and rule, he is not amenable to reason, he is self-assertive and intolerant, clings obstinately to his own opinions, has little sympathy or consideration for others, and is not calculated to make any woman happy.

A man who possesses a poor thumb, a crooked finger of Mercury, a hollow hand, with the fingers unevenly set, a long sloping Head-line, and the Mounts of Mars soft and low, is not likely to succeed in the world; he will allow himself to be pushed aside by others and trampled upon. He has no grit in him, and will sink under adversity, or require constant encouragement and help.

A man with long pointed fingers, narrow palm, weak thumb, Head and Heart lines close together, forming a narrow quadrangle, will be small-minded, discontented, and fault-finding. He will interfere in household matters not within his own province, and when he leaves his home there will probably be a sigh of relief as at the removal of a weight or heavy cloud. With short red nails also, he will be irritable and hard to please.

An ideal husband, as regards the home life, should have a long Heart-line with branches rising on to Jupiter, but not encircling the Mount; this will give him an affectionate nature. A straight finger of Jupiter (honour), a well developed, spatulate, or square, thumb with long first phalange (constancy). The Mounts of Luna and Venus must be well placed, but not too much in evidence; they give sympathy, benevolence, and a desire to please. Added to these signs of amiability, it would be well for him to have a clear deep Head-line, straight fingers, particularly that of Mercury; these denote the possession of common sense, sound judgment and ability. The indications of good health should also be present; these are, a firm hand with few lines, a good Life-line, and the lines of Head, Heart, and Hepatica normal.

It is essential that a man who is responsible for the comfort and welfare of a wife and family should have the powers that make for worldly success.

WOMEN'S HANDS AND MARRIAGE.

Any man who is anxious to escape from the loneliness or miseries of bachelorhood, who is truly seeking his spiritual affinity, and is not blinded by some overpowering fascination, may obtain an insight into the character of the girl who attracts him, before his attentions have become too pronounced, if he will study Palmistry, and make use of the knowledge it can give him. He will be able to find out the personal faults and failings which the restrictions of social intercourse and conventionalities of life enable her to hide; he will be able to penetrate the veneer of training and good breeding, and see the natural tastes and disposition; and possibly, in the search for flaws in the character, he may come across unsuspected depths of affection, strength of principle and endurance, capacities which may be unknown to the girl herself, the powers lying dormant until opportunity calls them forth, and in so doing a man may ensure his happiness, or avoid an ill-assorted alliance.

If a man desires a domesticated, helpful wife, let him choose a girl whose hand is a mixture of the spatulate and conic types; the palm being firm, the mounts well developed, the fingers straight and flexible, the Heart-line long, and the Mercury finger pointed. This shows an adaptable, tactful, affectionate disposition, useful but refined in feeling, and one who will make life happy for those around her, and who will find her own happiness in the home life.

Should a man want in his wife an intellectual companion, he will probably meet his requirements if he looks out for a woman with conic finger-tips or a mixture of square and pointed, or spatulate and pointed; the Mounts of Jupiter, Mercury, and Luna well developed, a clear deep Head-line sloping slightly. These signs indicate a thoughtful, intelligent, sympathetic, sociable disposition, other good qualities may of course accompany these, but the above are necessary for intellectual companionship.

If a man's desires do not soar beyond having a good housekeeper in his spouse, let him take a woman with long spatulate fingers, a firm hand, the third phalanges of all the fingers being thick, and the second and third knots developed. A hand of this kind denotes a good household manager, energetic, methodical and painstaking, and an excellent cook, but at the same time one who will have few ideas beyond the management of house and servants, and she may make home uncomfortable by too much fuss and attention to details.

If the aspirant after matrimony requires an ornamental charming wife, let him choose one whose hands are small, fingers pointed—Mercury finger particularly so, and the first phalange long—the Mounts of Venus and Apollo well developed, and the finger and Mount of Jupiter prominent. This combination denotes a very attractive nature. She will shine in society, have plenty to say, and, possessing tact and wheedling power, will probably turn him round her little finger, as the saying is. She will most likely also have beauty of face and form, but inward grace may be

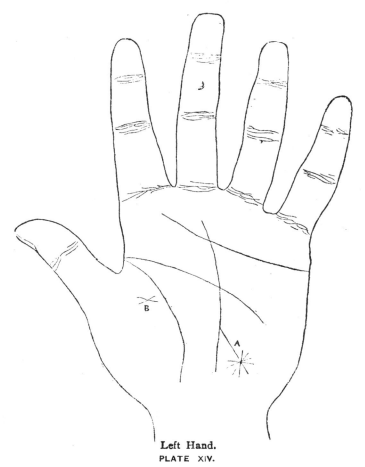

Left Hand.

PLATE XIV.

FROM PERSONAL EXPERIENCE.

(Marks on the hand of a girl whose fiancé committed suicide.)

A. The star on attachment-line signifies a shock in connection with that person.
B. Cross on the Mount of Mars under Jupiter,—— the sign of suicide. Being in the left hand it refers to some one belonging to "Subject," and does not indicate a personal attempt.

lacking, and in the hour of adversity she may prove a hindrance rather than a help.

A man does not care for a woman who poses as clever, independent and masterful, let him then avoid in his choice of a wife the woman whose hand is large, firm, fingers square and wide apart, the finger of Jupiter prominent and the Mount over-developed, while the other mounts are absent or very low, the thumb large, heavy, and knotted, the Head-line straight and the Heart-line short. There will be little sympathy or womanliness in this character. She will have a great opinion of herself, and will like to rule. She may be clever, but will have an unpleasant, ostentatious manner of showing it.

CHAPTER VII

On Choosing Employees or Domestic Servants

It is not always convenient or desirable to examine the hands of candidates for employment, but a casual glance may sometimes afford the information required.

A commercial traveller or agent employed to push any business, should possess a long, straight Mercury finger, with long first phalange, and a straight Head-line slightly forked. This will give him persuasive eloquence, he will be diplomatic in using people to his advantage, and quick in perceiving and using his opportunities. He should also have the Mount of Jupiter well developed, as he must be of a sociable nature.

If a confidential clerk is required, or any post of responsibility is to be filled, the applicant should have a straight finger of Jupiter, and a forked Heart-line. With these he will be thoroughly trustworthy, having a strong sense of honour and duty. The fingers should not be too much outspread, or he will not be able to keep a secret. With a high Mount of Mars (under Mercury) he will be reserved in disposition and may be trusted not to betray confidences.

A lady engaging a cook would do well to look first at the fingers of the person applying for the situation. The third phalanges of all the fingers should be rather thick, and the second knots present, in which case she will not be guided by " the rule of thumb," but will weigh and measure carefully, and do all work in a regular, methodical manner. Should she have a long prominent finger of Jupiter, a heavy thumb, and short square nails, it will be well to let her have her own way, if peace is desired, as she will brook no interference in her domain

H

A **housemaid** should have straight spatulate fingers and firm palm. With these points she will be active and conscientious. If she has a soft palm she will probably be lazy in getting up in the morning, and the work will be done in a hurry, or left undone altogether.

A **nurse** should have spatulate fingers, and the Mount of Apollo encroaching on Mercury, a good Heart-line, and well-developed Mount of Venus. This will give her activity, gentleness, a love of children and all things young and tender, and she will also have the art of pleasing. If the fingers are short, the nails small and red or square at the base, the finger of Jupiter crooked, the Heart-line short and without branches, the hand flat and hard, and the Mounts of Apollo and Venus low, the children in her charge are greatly to be pitied. She will have no patience with them, and will vent her own bad temper upon their helplessness.

A girl of the working class with pointed fingers will not do well in domestic service, unless as lady's maid. She will make a good milliner, florist, or assistant in any light trade. She is fastidious, and does not care for rough or hard work, but if Mercury is dominant in her hand she will make a good needle-woman.

A **coachman's hand** should be spatulate or square, the palm broad and unlined, the Mounts of Mars good, and the Mount of Apollo leaning towards Mercury. With which indications he will have courage, presence of mind, and he will treat his horses kindly.

With these few suggestions I shall leave my readers to work out further for themselves the qualities that are essential to the various employments of civilised life, with the corresponding signs to be found in Palmistry.

CHAPTER VIII

Palmistry as a Society Amusement

THE human race is, above all things, egotistic. We like to be the **centre of interest,** to discourse upon ourselves, to make others listen to accounts of our adventures, experiences, woes, and grievances. And we love to be talked about; criticism even is not unwelcome so long as it lifts us out of obscurity ! " Superior " people may scoff, but few can restrain their curiosity when the **search-light of Palmistry** is turned upon themselves.

As a **drawing-room entertainment** Palmistry never fails. Hostesses sometimes engage the best artistes it is possible to procure, and find they are deserted for the Palmist's corner ! Of course it is " fortune-telling " that draws the crowd, **people want to know** " what is going to happen to them," and all desire that " something " to be unalloyed bliss, unbounded wealth, and the gratification of every wish ! And it is curious to notice how in the minds of some people the seer is connected with the forecast, as if the Palmist had the power to bring about, or avert, the fulfilment of the prophecy.

We have seen that it is only possible to a certain extent to read the future. **We can see possibilities and probabilities, but no more.** Therefore when **fortune-telling** is indulged in it must not be taken too seriously, and no one should allow the predictions of palmist, clairvoyant or other, to influence or direct his life, if not in accordance with his own good sense and judgment. To follow blindly any advice given is foolish in the extreme. At the same time warnings should not be disregarded.

In using the cult of Palmistry simply as an entertainment it is wise to dwell mostly upon the lighter and brighter side, to keep as much as possible to character-reading, leaving events alone, although these are what arrest the attention and interest the " subject."

When surrounded by a crowd of listeners, the faults of character must not be too severely dealt with. A man may not mind at a private audience confessing his shortcomings, but he naturally does not like the process of being publicly turned inside out, and the failings unveiled which he fondly hopes lie concealed within him, and this in the presence of some whose good opinion he values, and fears to lose.

There is no occasion, however, to flatter and pass over all blemishes of character ; there are many ways of putting an unpleasant truth. Faults may be pointed out in such a manner as not to give offence or hurt the feelings. A particular propensity may be hinted at, which will be quite sufficient for a sensitive nature, and a self-satisfied person with blunted perception will not see or own his failings even when clearly pointed out.

Warnings in regard to health may be given, but too much detail would be out of place, and undesired by the " subject."

Past events, when of a nature that can be alluded to in general company, may be brought forward, as these afford proof of the genuineness of the science, and awaken an interest in it.

The talents and tastes, occupations and pursuits that the hand displays should be made much of— this is safe ground, and interesting as well—and when the "subject" is seen to be in a position for which he is unfit, the proper direction for the development of his powers and gifts may be pointed out.

The dates at which certain events or changes have occurred should be mentioned—this is considered a wonderful demonstration of the capabilities of the system. Statements of events may be pure guess-work, but to fix upon the actual age at which they took place is something more.

On no account should the date of death be foretold. In the first place it is impossible with certainty to do so; in the second, it is unwise to implant in impressionable, sensitive minds the thought that their doom is unalterably fixed, an idea which, perhaps, when illness comes, will take from them all hope of recovery, and the effort necessary to shake off the evil.

So also in regard to insanity. If evidence of the inheritance of such a disease is present, or if there are any signs of failing mental powers, the knowledge must be withheld. Much harm has ensued from the rashness of amateur Palmists in foretelling terrible calamities. If pressed to disclose the view of the possible future—as often occurs when curiosity overcomes discretion—it should be the Palmist's rule to say as little as possible of coming evils, unless a method of avoiding these can be indicated at the same time. It is better not to know beforehand the sorrows that must befall us.

In the case of marriage, when the signs are undoubtedly unpropitious, if the step has not been taken, it is advisable to give a warning—to remark that the "subject" would be happier single—or if bent upon matrimony, to caution him or her to exercise judgment, not to enter rashly and hurriedly into an engagement, and to be guided only by the highest principles and motives.

Certain people are more liable to **accidents** than others, there seems to be a fatality about them, and the type to which the individual belongs will indicate the nature of the special danger to be avoided. For example :—Saturnians (people in whose hands the finger and Mount of Saturn are most prominent) are subject to falls and accidents which affect the lower limbs. A preponderance of Luna's influence renders the person unsafe on water. When this is apparent on the hand the Palmist is justified in giving the warning, but **should never pronounce it as a doom.**

There are methods of forecasting the future in regard to **love and marriage** which may cause much interest and entertainment, but these, it must be understood, are as yet entirely experimental, and have not been accepted as reliable, but if taken as distinct from proven rules, they may be practised without harm. Thus :—The **personal appearance** of the possible lover, wife, or husband can be described through the presence of fine hair-lines rising from the "influence-line" to one of the mounts, from which characteristics and probable tastes and occupations can be inferred. These, if not applicable to the real partner, will at least portray an influence present in the life, or the ideal formed by the mind, the kind of person that would be most attractive to the "subject" (see chapter on "The Types, their Personal Appearance, Character and Tastes").

Letters and other symbols are also found upon the hand, the former often applying to people who influence the life. They may be friends, relatives, or enemies, according to the mounts and lines on

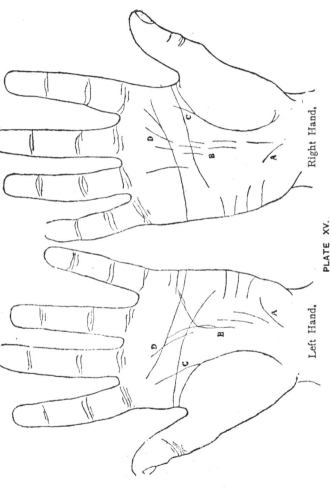

Left Hand.

Right Hand.

PLATE XV.

From Personal Experience.

Changes marked on the Fate-line. "Subject," a man aged 33, had never settled long at one employment.

A. Fate-line turning to Lunar. He went to Africa at an early age. There he changed his occupation several times.

B. Island on Fate line and on line from Mercury, "influence line" denotes that one change about the age of 30 was caused by an unhappy attachment.

C. Fresh start in life.

D. Fate line going towards Jupiter promises success.

which they appear. These are frequently read in advance of the events with which they are connected. The affinities, too, of the different types for each other will assist in the delineation of the character and description of the possible or probable mate, but it must only be considered a suggestion, not a certainty.

If the exponent of Palmistry is endeavouring seriously to demonstrate the science, it is best to see the "subject" alone. The result will be far more satisfactory to both parties, and the difficulties for the Palmist will be considerably lessened.

A flat denial of what is plainly written upon the hand is frequently a stumbling-block, and this is sometimes given simply because the "subject" did not expect the secret or fault would be discovered, and had not the moral courage to own it before his friends. Without an audience he will admit the truth, and often help the Palmist by maintaining a passive mind instead of an antagonistic one, such as would be roused in self-defence when put, in public, under the dissecting knife.

The influence of other minds also hinders a correct delineation if the Palmist be "sensitive," that is, susceptible to impressions, or thought-transference, and these "brain-waves" occasionally mislead and confuse a Palmist who is not strong enough to throw them off.

In private all sorts of confidences are given to the Palmist who ought to respect these as doctors do, and it is in such cases that, if discreet, he can help and comfort a fellow-creature, cheering a broken spirit, pointing out the path of amendment, or showing the direction wherein hope lies.

CHAPTER IX

The Types, Their Personal Appearance, Character and Tastes

THE most superficial character-reader must have observed how certain temperaments accord with the complexion and general personal appearance of the individual. Fair-haired people are usually of a bright, sunny, sanguine nature. Those with red-hair and florid complexion are hasty, passionate and headstrong. Dark-haired people are serious, sometimes melancholy. People with brown hair and eyes have great warmth of affection. Grey-eyed people are clever as a rule, but the disposition is cold. Working out this principle, to each type in Palmistry, certain characteristics have, after careful observation, been assigned, and these will be found in most instances correct.

When in a hand the finger and Mount of Jupiter are more prominent than any of the others, its possessor is said to be of the type of Jupiter, and his character, actions, tastes and pursuits will be influenced for good or evil, by the qualities belonging to that class.

We have seen that pure types are rarely met with, and a hand will frequently give evidence of two over-mastering influences. The "subject" will then be found to have some of the characteristics of each, opposing qualities perhaps, which will modify or counteract the effect. I shall, however, only describe the attributes and so forth, of the pure types; the blending of these the student will, with practice, discover for himself, and with a clue here and there he will be able to form a very fair judgment of the individual.

PERSONAL APPEARANCE OF JUPITERIANS.

Jupiterians are strong, of medium height and grow stout as they get older. They have clear complexions, often with slight colour. Large penetrating, grey or light blue eyes. The nose is straight, well-formed and has a high bridge. The mouth is well proportioned, with teeth large and white, the two central ones being conspicuous. The chin is square with a cleft or dimple in the centre. The throat is full and well-formed. Their hair is fine, chestnut coloured, and inclined to curl, it is abundant in youth, but Jupiterians grow bald early. Their ears are of medium size and lie close to the head. Their voices are clear, pleasant, but commanding. Their hands are large and flexible, the first finger being particularly prominent. The thumb is generally strong, giving the power to rule, which is one of the great desires of a Jupiterian. They are graceful in movement, and always dress well.

Character.

Pronounced Jupiterians are above all things ambitious, they like to take the lead, and to occupy prominent positions. They are usually clever and successful. They are rather conventional, and have great respect for law, order and constitutional government. In religion they like display and ceremony. As friends they are sincere, chivalrous, and ready to help, but prefer to subscribe to public charities, " to be known of men," and do not give anonymously. They are proud and self-confident, straightforward, good-natured and generous. Justice and benevolence are also among their favourable qualities.

Excess in all things is bad, so when there is an

over-development of any trait of character, the effect is to nullify or pervert its good influence, thus an ill-balanced Jupiterian is selfish, conceited, ostentatious, given to boasting and vulgar display. He is improvident, self-indulgent, lacking religious feeling and honour.

Tastes and Pursuits.

Jupiterians are gregarious. They are fond of social intercourse, and shine in society, taking pains to make themselves agreeable. They are excellent hosts, and enjoy the pleasures of the table. Their intellectual tastes incline them to literature, especially to biographies, history and romance. In travelling they will spend most of their time in cities, and in visiting places of entertainment, or scenes of former festivity. They do not care for solitude or the lonely mountain path; however beautiful the landscape they will enjoy it only when in company. From preference they become teachers, lawyers, clergymen, and public officials. In all professions, or callings, a Jupiterian will lead, not follow. Should he enter the army he will probably distinguish himself by his powers of good generalship, and rise in rank, or he will make himself disliked by his self-assertion and overbearing conceit.

The shape of the hands must also be taken into account. A Jupiterian with square fingers will, when he leads or rules, do so with deliberation and after reasoning the matter out. If his fingers are pointed or conic, he will judge intuitively of what is right and wrong, wise or judicious, and he will encourage people to follow his lead more by persuasion than by argument. With spatulate fingers his personal action and example will attract adherents.

A prominent Mount of Jupiter in a musical hand will give a taste for sacred music. The organ, or harmonium, will be the chosen instrument. In an artist's hand, the influence of Jupiter will incline him to brilliant colouring, the favourite colour being red.

SATURNIANS.

People having a strong influence of Saturn in their composition are tall, thin, with stooping shoulders. They are slow in movement and walk with an unsteady gait, their toes turning in. They have sallow complexions and small, black, deeply set eyes. The eyebrows are close together and well marked. The nose is long, pointed and turns down. The mouth is large and the lips thin ; the teeth are large, good and white, but decay early and cause much suffering. Their jaws are large and massive, and they have long chins. The ears are large and close to the head, the hair is straight, long, thick and black. They have long thin necks, high cheek bones, and their hands are large and bony, with prominent knuckles and long fingers. Their voices are hoarse, monotonous and low. They usually wear black or neutral tints. They have little pleasure in fine garments, and are careless of personal appearance.

Character.

The influence of Saturn imparts gravity and depth to the character. The favourable development of Saturn renders the " subject " contemplative, reserved, patient and studious. He is sincere in friendship, devout in religion, but is bigoted and intolerant. He is economical, prudent, steady and fond of home. His judgment is sound, he is cool and calculating, inclined to be distrustful and apprehensive, he will err on the side of caution and has no desire for speculation. Although strict regarding his own life he is tolerant of other people's actions. He is methodical and regular in his ways, and dislikes all innovation, or upsetting of the daily routine. He is not fond of society, makes few friends and passes much of his time alone.

When ill-balanced the Saturnian is selfish, peevish, envious and suspicious. He is obstinate, argumentative and inclined to provoke quarrels. **A dangerous enemy,** for he is cunning, crafty and revengeful; for while the attributes of Saturn are necessary for the formation of a well-balanced nature, the Saturnian qualities in excess are more pernicious than any other.

Tastes and Pursuits.

Saturnians are fond of **music and mathematics,** and often have a talent for invention. They become mathematicians, agriculturists, estate agents, printers and sometimes Low Church clergymen. They take an interest in antiquities, mummies, weapons with which crimes have been committed, instruments of torture, and anything of similar description. Their tastes are morbid, and they like dull and dingy fabrics. In a musician's hand Saturn will give a preference for the violin and rhymic measure. In a painter's hand a partiality for sombre colouring and sad pictures.

APOLLO.

The subjects of Apollo are endowed with bright **cheerful natures,** a love of art and beauty. They are intelligent more than clever, their ideas are clear and their perceptions quick.

Appearance.

Medium height, but well proportioned. **Good-looking as a rule.** They have round prominent foreheads, fair or golden hair, which is bright, soft and abundant. Their features are clearly cut. The nose is straight, the mouth medium-sized and well formed, chin prominent and rounded. ᴥ They have well-opened blue or brown eyes, with long, dark, curled-up eyelashes. The ears are medium-sized and lie close to the head. Teeth are even, but not very white. They have transparent skins, with a little red in the cheeks, which are dimpled. Their movements are graceful, and their manners charming. Their voices are pure, sweet, musical and soothing. Their hands are fine and fingers supple, the tips and nails are of different shapes.

Character.

A favourable influence of Apollo gives to its subject **benevolence** and generosity, a nature free from superstition, and tolerant of creeds and opinions that differ from his own. He is honest, proud and just. He scorns meanness, and is free with his money. He is effusive with his thanks, but forgets quickly. He is always courteous and pleasant, but he likes other people to work for him, being of an indolent nature. When ill-balanced he is frivolous, quick-tempered and selfish. Fickle in love and changeable in friendship. Extravagant and reckless. He is fond of money, is ostentatious, boastful and self-satisfied.

Tastes and Pursuits.

The subject of Apollo is fond of artistic surroundings, and likes religious services to be bright and musical. His favourite colour is yellow. He will

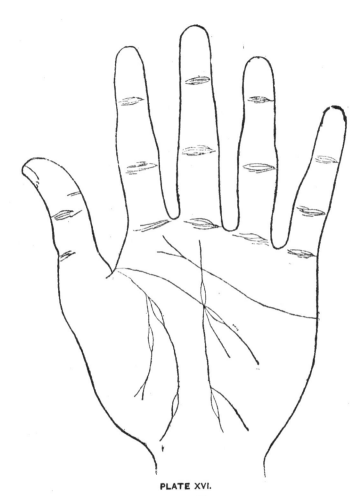

PLATE XVI.

FROM PERSONAL EXPERIENCE.

Combination of Islands. Seen in the hand of lady of high social position. Primary cause—unhappy attachment after marriage. Health affected thereby.

choose the profession of chemist, doctor, actor, or any pursuit connected with art, literature or science.

The influence of Apollo gives an instinct for colouring true to nature, the taste for calm, sedate inspiring music, and the love of beautiful paintings, statues, delicate laces and fabrics, and artistic furniture.

MERCURY.

For success in business and life generally it is well to have a strong finger of Mercury and good mount, without these, or rather the qualities they represent, the struggle for existence will be much harder. Mercury gives intelligence, penetration, aptitude for business, and the capacity for making use of talents, opportunities, and people.

Appearance.

Mercurians are of small stature, with well-made figures, and their movements are quick and light. They preserve a youthful appearance to a late age. Their faces are very expressive, their mouths being extremely mobile, the lips are thin and slightly open, showing small regular teeth. The chin is pointed. Their eyes, brown or dark blue, are restless, penetrating and deep-set. The forehead is high and prominent, and the nose straight. Complexion is soft and fair, of a slightly yellow shade, and the colour in their cheeks changes with every passing emotion. Their hair is cl a ut but with changing shades and a reddish tint, and curls slightly. Their hands are long and supple, and the finger-tips are of different shapes. The finger of Mercury is pointed and long in proportion to the others. Their voices are rather weak, but their utterance is rapid, and they sometimes stammer.

Character.

Mercurians are industrious, talkative, restless, intelligent, hopeful. They are thoughtful and quick-witted, full of tact and discrimination. They are somewhat clannish, and will help their own people even when these are undeserving, but are hospitable to strangers. Their memories are good, they have logical minds, and are not credulous. It is difficult to get the better of a Mercurian, for he is always on the alert, and has quick penetration and intuition.

A badly-balanced Mercurian is indiscreet, untruthful, crafty and malicious. He has propensities for thieving, and unscrupulously using people and circumstances for his own advantage. His temper is passionate and ungovernable.

Tastes and Pursuits.

Mercurians frequently display a taste for science, and a talent for writing. They become doctors, lawyers, authors, teachers, clerks, accountants and booksellers. They often take up the business of stockbroker or merchant, and are clever with their fingers. Their favourite colour is green. The music they prefer is that of comic or light opera. They collect curiosities of all kinds.

MARS.

People of Martian temperament are unconventional, courageous and full of energy.

Appearance.

They are of middle height, strong and square-shouldered. They are quick and brusque in manner and movement. They have small heads, rather thick necks, and hard, dry, red skins. Their foreheads are high, and the hair, which grows back from the temples, is red in colour, coarse in texture and curly. Their eyes are brown, with a reddish shade, wide open, and the whites are often blood-shot. The eyebrows are close to the eyes and bushy. The mouth is large and the lips are thick. The teeth are short and yellowish in colour. The chin is massive and square. The ears are large and stand out from the head. The nose is aquiline. Their voices are loud, coarse and domineering. Their hands are hard, with thick fingers, and the Mounts of Mars firm and high.

Character.

Mars gives a great amount of aggressiveness and courage. A Martian can always fight his own battles, and enjoys contest. He has something of the bulldog nature, faithful but fierce. He is matter-of-fact, and does not understand sentiment. He is generous, persevering, cool in the face of danger, and acts promptly. He is hasty in temper, and cannot bear restraint.

Mars ill-balanced becomes cruel, headstrong and vicious. Ill-regulated Martians are liable to become drunkards, and lead restless, unsettled lives. They frequent low company, and their tastes are coarse.

Tastes and Pursuits.

A Martian enjoys a life of noise and turmoil. He is fond of riding, hunting, and sports of all kinds, and has a partiality for dogs and horses. He likes travelling, and living out of doors. He does not readily settle down to domesticity. Martians from choice become soldiers, sailors, explorers, sportsmen, and will take up any occupation connected with horses, and will engage in any enterprise in which there is an element of personal danger. They like strong vivid colours,

bright red and purple are their favourites. A
Martian has the fancy for collecting armour and
weapons of every description, or anything connected with warfare. The books he reads are
romances with stirring incidents, tales of the battle-
field and so on. In music he likes energetic and
inspiring airs, and has a preference for brass
instruments.

LUNA.

Luna gives to her subjects imagination, a love
of solitude and day-dreaming. There is much
melancholy and poetic sentiment in their composition. They are morbidly apprehensive, and
become hypochondriacs. They like mysticism,
and often have prophetic dreams.

Appearance.

Lunar subjects are tall with muscular, loosely-
knit figures. They have round heads with long,
straight, colourless hair of fine texture. Their skin
is pale and soft. Their foreheads are prominent
over the eyebrows, and broad at the temples.
Their eyes are large, either grey or blue and have
a languid expression. The eyebrows meet over
the nose and are lightly marked. Their mouths
are small, but the lips are full and slightly open.
The teeth are large, yellow and irregular. The
chin is rounded and retreating. The nose is short.
Their voices are low and unanimated. Their hands
are soft, white and plump, with long, pointed fingers,
short thumbs, and a high Mount of Luna.

Character.

They are very unpractical people, dreamy,
idealistic, and poetical. They are noble, heroic,
and emotional, but sympathetic and gentle. They
are inconstant and swayed by the mood of the
moment.

The influence of Luna perverted makes a hypocritical, deceitful, jealous character. An unreasonable, discontented, superstitious being, and one whose mental equilibrium is easily disturbed and over-balanced.

Tastes and Pursuits.

Luna subjects have a **liking for literature,** and they sometimes write, but will do nothing more practical. They dislike commerce and will only go into business if their head-line is very straight. They are fond of art, but of a fantastic nature. They are given to collecting old china and curios, crystals, shells, grotesque figures, and unnatural things. The colours they prefer are sea-green, silvery-grey, and very pale tints. In music they like harmony more than melody, and have a partiality for the clarionet, flute, and all wind instruments.

VENUS.

The subjects of Venus are endowed with **beauty of person and charm of manner.** They appreciate all the pleasures of the senses. They are tender, loving, and desire to be loved. They are demonstrative and attractive.

Appearance.

They are **small in size,** inclining to stoutness. They have beautiful complexions and their skin is soft, white and delicate. Their faces are round, and their eyes are large and clear, brown in colour and have a liquid look. The eyebrows are dark and beautifully pencilled. The nose is small and well-shaped, but slightly *retroussé*. Their mouths are small, the lips red, well-formed and dimpled at the corners. The teeth are small, white and regular. Their hair is long, thick, soft and wavy, brown or

black, and does not change with age. The ears
are small, pink, shapely and lie close to the head.
The cheeks and chin are soft, round and dimpled.
Their voices are sweet, soft, but drawling. Their
hands are small, plump, and dimpled, fingers
smooth and pointed with the third phalanges thick.

Character.

They are cultured, good-natured, self-sacrificing
and full of sympathy. They dislike noise and fuss,
and are easily moved to tears. They delight in
pleasure and love to be admired.

An excess of Venus will make the individual
selfish, sensual, exacting, fond of dress and eating
and drinking, self-indulgent, regardless of consequences as long as the desire of the moment is
gratified.

Tastes and Pursuits.

They are fond of painting, of music, singing and
elocution. They love travelling, and have a weakness for dress and jewellery. They become
musicians, actors and artists of all kinds. They
love to collect jewels, lace, amorous paintings, silky
fabrics, and they delight in flowers and perfumes.
Their favourite colours are rose and blue. In
music they incline more to melody than harmony,
and the instrument they prefer is the violoncello.

THE AFFINITIES.

"Extremes Meet," and in so doing supply
deficiencies of character, or support the weaker as
the case may be. Mercurial people attract those
of the temperament of Luna. Saturn and Apollo,
being of opposite natures, are magnetically drawn to
one another. Mars and Venus have a liking for
each other. Jupiter, being of a social disposition, is
friendly with each and all.

INDEX

SOME HANDBOOKS
ON
USEFUL HOBBIES.

Carpentry and Cabinet-making

An Illustrated Handbook for the Amateur, with numerous Drawings and Designs,

By W. M. OAKWOOD.

Cloth, **Price 1s.**, *post free* **1s. 2d.**

This handbook contains a description of the tools most generally used, with instructions how to use them—The choice of woods for various purposes—Fretwork as applied to cabinet-making—A chapter on French polishing, staining, and varnishing.

Wood Carving
A Practical Guide for the Home Student.

By J. H. GARNETT.

With numerous Illustrations & Designs.

Cloth, **Price 1s.**, *post free* **1s. 2d.**

Contains—in addition to all instruction on the practice of the art of Wood-Carving—Chapters on Choice of Woods, Tools, Designs, Appliances, etc., Chip or Notch Carving, Staining, Polishing, Gilding, Painting, etc.

Metal Work

A Practical Handbook for the Amateur Worker in Iron, Brass, Zinc, Copper, etc.

By GEORGE DAY, F.R.M.S.

With numerous Illustrations & Designs.

Cloth, **Price 1s.**, *post free* **1s. 2d.**

Some of the 16 Chapters are — Tools required for Metal-work—General Methods of Copying the pattern, drawing and transferring—General Methods of Working—To Etch on Metals—Fretworking in Metals—Useful Recipes for Metals and Metal Workers, etc., etc.

Stamp Collecting for Pleasure and Profit

A Simple Guide through the highways and byways of Philately.

By CECIL H. BULLIVANT, Author of "The Drawing Room Entertainer," etc.

Cloth, **Price 1s.** *net, post free* **1s. 3d.**

Contents:—How to begin a Collection—The Album and Catalogue—Perforations and Watermarks—Fakes and Forgeries—Stamps of Great Price and "Errors"—"Famous Finds," etc., etc.

How to Take and Fake Photographs

By CLIVE HOLLAND.

Cloth, with 8 full-page Illustrations.

Price 1s., *post free* **1s. 2d.**

The Contents include :—The Dark Room—Cameras, Plates and Films—The Selection of Subjects—Exposure—Development and after Treatment of Negatives—Printing Processes—Mounting—Competition and Exhibition Work, etc., etc.

Basket Making at Home

By MARY WHITE.

With 12 Illustrations and many Diagrams

Price 1s. *net, post free* **1s. 3d.**

The Contents include :—Raffia and some of its uses—Weaving a Small Basket—Covered Basket—Baskets with Handles — Some Work Baskets—Sweet Baskets—Waste Paper Baskets—Dolls, Furniture—Caning in a Frame or on a Chair, etc., etc.

Model Making

By CYRIL HALL.

With Illustrations and Working Designs.

Price 1s. *net, post free* **1s. 3d.**

The volume includes practical instruction for the making of a Steam Locomotive — Turbine Steam Boat — Electric Engine—Motors—Yachts—Printing Press—Steam Crane — Telephone — Electric Bell — Telegraph, etc., etc.

Half-Hours with the Microscope

A Popular Guide to the Use of the Microscope as a Means of Amusement and Instruction.

By EDWIN LANKESTER, M.D.

With Eight Plates.

Cloth, **Price 1s.**, *post free* **1s. 2d.**

CONTENTS.—A Half-hour on each of the following topics :—The Structure of the Microscope — In the Garden — In the Country—At the Pond Side—At the Sea Side—Indoors—Polarized Light.

The above volumes may be had of all Booksellers, or post-free from the Publishers,
C. Arthur Pearson, Ltd., 17-18 Henrietta Street, London, W.C. 2.

USEFUL HANDBOOKS ON
The GARDEN & HOME PETS

Small Gardens
And How to Make the Most of Them.

By VIOLET P. BIDDLE. *Cloth.*
Price 1s., *post free* **1s. 2d.**

A most useful Handbook for the Amateur. Full instructions are given for laying-out, bedding, arrangement of borders, vegetable culture, flowers and fruit, and trees, room plants, window boxes, etc.

SMALL GARDENS AND HOW TO MAKE THE MOST OF THEM BY VIOLET BIDDLE

The Market Garden
How to Start and Run it Profitably.

With numerous Illustrations.
By the Gardening Experts of "The Smallholder."

Stiff Wrapper, **Price 1s.** *net, post free* **1s. 3d.**

"There is a large amount of thoroughly useful information to be gleaned from its pages, and it is wonderful value for the money."—*Field.*
"An excellent little handbook."—*Rural World.*
"Contains sound and practical advice."—*Farm and Home.*

Greenhouses
How to Make and Manage Them.

By WILLIAM F. ROWLES.
With numerous Diagrams.

Cloth, **Price 1s.,** *post free* **1s. 2d.**

Some of the 22 Chapters deal with:—House Construction—The Heating Question—Working up Stock—Propagation—Pots and Potting—Soils and Manures—Watering—Shading—Tying and Staking—Syringing—Training—Pinching and Pruning—Arranging—Forcing—Critical Periods in Plant Life—Specialisation, etc., etc.

The Hobby Gardener

By A. C. MARSHALL, F.R.H.S.
With 22 full-page Illustrations.
In Stiff Three-coloured Cover.

Price 1s. *net, post free* **1s. 3d.**

The work in the garden for each month of the year is shown by pictures and instruction. Everything is clearly explained so that the novice can soon acquire the necessary skill and knowledge to keep the garden bright.

THE DOG
In Health and Disease

By F. M. ARCHER.
With 12 Illustrations.

By S. T. DADD, *Cloth,*
Price 1s., *post free* **1s. 2d.**

THE DOG IN HEALTH & DISEASE
BY F. M. ARCHER

Cage and Singing Birds

By GEORGE GARDNER.
With numerous Illustrations.

Cloth, **Price 1s.,** *post free* **1s. 2d.**

CAGE AND SINGING BIRDS
GEORGE GARDNER

Some of the Contents are :—Birds for Song, for Exhibition, and for Breeding—Care of young—Seeds how and what to buy—Moulting for song and for exhibition—Colour-feeding: how it is done—Diseases of Cage Birds and how to treat them—Bird fever — Parasites and how to destroy them, etc., etc.

The above volumes may be had of all Booksellers, or post-free from the Publishers,
C. Arthur Pearson, Ltd., 17-18 Henrietta Street, London, W.C. 2.

PRACTICAL HANDBOOKS
on
HOME MANAGEMENT.

Small Homes and How to Furnish Them

By EDITH WALDEMAR LEVERTON.

With 16 Illustrations.

Cloth, **Price 1s.**, *post free* **1s. 2d.**

Contents :—
Choosing the Home—The Furniture — Wall Papers—Floor Coverings —Red, Blue, Green, Yellow and Pink Rooms —The Entrance Hall— Staircase Nooks — Cosy Sitting Rooms — The Dining Room — Kitchen Scullery—The Bedrooms, etc.

Home Making
A Book of Practical Household Hints.
By S. E. STONE.

Crown 8vo, Cloth, **Price 1s.**, *net*.

This work embraces the whole art of keeping the home in good order, from kitchen to garret, and thus ensuring, if its advice is carried out, the health and comfort of the whole family.

House Taking and House Holding
By WILLIAM BLAIR.

Cloth, **Price 1s.**, *post free* **1s. 2d.**

This useful volume contains 33 chapters, dealing, amongst other things, with the Choice of a House, Sub-soils, Leases, Repairing Leases, Sanitation, Removal, Rates and Taxes, Furnished Houses, Fixtures, Flats, Maisonettes, Insurance, Nuisances, etc., etc.

How to Keep House on £200 a Year
By MRS. PRAGA.

Author of " Dinners of the Day," etc.

Crown 8vo, Cloth, **Price 1s.**, *post free* **1s. 2d.**

PART I. contains 16 chapters on the Choice and Management of a Home.
PART II. contains 8 chapters on How to Furnish the Home.
PART III. contains 9 chapters on Household Duties and Arrangements.

How to Live Well on Five Shillings a Week per Head
By L. RUTHERFORD SKEY.

Cloth, **Price 1s.** *net*, *post free* **1s. 3d.**

The Contents include :— Unconsidered Trifles—Breakfast and Supper Dishes—Meat, What to Buy, and How to Cook It—Substitutes for Meat—Fish—Soups and the Stock-Pot—Fruit and Vegetables — Puddings—How to Spend the Five Shillings; Tables of Daily Expenditure—Five Shillings a Week in the Country—Recipes, &c.

" The suggestions of how the innumerable unconsidered trifles which, in the menage of the poor as well as the rich, are promptly consigned to the dust-bin, may be utilised are so practical and so true that, on their account alone, the purchaser of this little volume, packed with sound and simple facts buys a very good shillingsworth."

Household Hints
Edited by
" ISOBEL," of *Home Notes*.

Price 1s., *post free* **1s. 2d.**

This Volume deals with every kind of Advice and Recipe for keeping a House in perfect condition.

Plain Needlework
Edited by
" ISOBEL," of *Home Notes*.

Cloth, **Price 1s.**, *post free* **1s. 2d.**

The object of this book is to show, by examples and simple directions, the best way of executing all the most necessary details of what is usually termed plain work.

To those who wish to instruct their children or pupils to sew, this book will prove most useful.

The above volumes may be had of all Booksellers, or post-free from the Publishers,
C. Arthur Pearson, Ltd., 17-18 Henrietta Street, London, W.C. 2.

USEFUL HANDBOOKS ON
COOKERY.

Cold Meat
And How to Disguise It.
By M. G. RATTRAY.
Diploma of the National Training School of Cookery.

Cloth,
Price 1s.,
post free
1s. 2d.

Contains a number of Useful Recipes for the Serving of Cold Meat in an Appetising Manner.

Little French Dinners
By EVELEEN DE RIVAZ.
("EVE.")

Cloth, **Price 1s.** *net, post free,* **1s. 3d.**

This excellent book contains Thirty Choice Menu, besides chapters on Savoury Toasts, the Use of Stale Bread, Seasonable Salads, Fancy Salads, Cooking Macaroni, etc., etc.

Breakfast and Supper Dishes
By C. H. SENN.

Cloth,
Price 1s.,
post free
1s. 2d.

The Recipes include Fish, Meat, etc., Vegetables, Salads, etc., Eggs, Omelettes, etc., Farinaceous and Cheese Dishes, etc., etc.

Dainty Dishes
for Slender Incomes
EDITED BY
"ISOBEL," of *Home Notes*

Cloth, **Price 1s.,** *post free* **1s. 2d.**

The Contents include Soups, Garnishes, Fish, Sauces, Entrées, Removes, Vegetables, Sweets, Savouries, Artizan Cookery, Cakes, Food Calendar, etc.

Vegetarian Cookery
EDITED BY
"ISOBEL," of *Home Notes.*

Cloth, **Price 1s.,** *post free* **1s. 2d**

Some of the Contents are:—General Remarks on Vegetarian Faré — General Remarks on Vegetables — Soups — Simple Vegetable Recipes — Entrées and Savouries — Farinaceous and Cheese — Eggs — Omelets — Curries — Macaroni — Liaisons and Sauces — Salads, etc.

Little Economies
And How to Practise Them.
By EDITH WALDEMAR LEVERTON.

Cloth, **Price 1s.,** *post free* **1s. 2d.**

Contents:—
General Management — The Financial Question — Kitchen Economies — Cooking Economies — Fuel, Firing and Lights — Catering — Home-made Jams, Pickles, etc. — The Kitchen Garden — Poultry Keeping — Laundry Work — Carving — Entertaining — The Servant Question — Spring Cleaning — Floral Decoration — Home Carpentering — The Sick Room — The Care of Clothes — Home Dressing, etc., etc.

The above volumes may be had of all Booksellers, or post-free from the Publishers, C. Arthur Pearson, Ltd., 17-18 Henrietta Street, London, W.C. 2.